EMPLOYEE PUBLICATIONS

*Theory and Practice of Communications
in the Modern Organization*

EMPLOYEE PUBLICATIONS

Theory and Practice of Communications
in the Modern Organization

WILLIAM C. HALLEY

CHILTON COMPANY—BOOK DIVISION
Publishers

Philadelphia - - - - - - - - *New York*

132437

LIBRARY OF CONGRESS CATALOG CARD NUMBER 59–9467

MANUFACTURED IN THE UNITED STATES OF AMERICA
BY QUINN & BODEN COMPANY, INC., RAHWAY, N. J.

Preface

The transmission of news and ideas fills a basic need wherever a group of people share a common environment or interests. This need is satisfied alike by neighborhood gossip, the prison grapevine, the public address system of a warship, or the journals of learned societies.

In business and industry, the "need to know" is increasingly satisfied by one of the most remarkable phenomena of the years since World War II: the new and lusty press of the sponsored, management-produced "company publication."

Beamed largely to employees and conceived essentially as a tool to promote organizational harmony, this press began as a tiny trickle of newspapers and magazines in the thirties. Today, it has swelled to a flood whose combined per-issue circulation is about six times larger than U.S. daily newspaper coverage, and 11 times larger than the combined circulations of *Life, Look, Reader's Digest, The Saturday Evening Post,* and *Time.*

Such rapid growth from such humble beginnings is impressive. As might be expected, however, the employee periodical is a blend of child and adult and suffers from the adolescent's growing pains. Thus far, it has had little time to develop fixed standards and guideposts. There is little literature and no body of tradition to point directions. The training and selection of editorial personnel remains on a hit-or-miss basis. The average "house organ," compared with its ultimate development, may well be as yet in the pioneering stage.

The field's weaknesses have been widely publicized. Throughout the years that employee publications have been multiplying, their management-sponsors have received continuous advice from critics both inside and outside the field. Personnel men, business journals, consultants—all have had their innings. The most prevalent general criticism advanced is that the content of most employee periodicals is "innocuous." That is, too much space, time, and money are lavished on the personal, trivial, or noncontroversial news tidbit at the expense of serious discussion of matters significant to industrial relations and the welfare of employees and management alike.

This general charge is undoubtedly true. But a problem rises when a typical plant or company management tries to find a widely shared definition of "significant, substantial content." To one commentator, "substance" may mean that management should continuously print articles designed to impress employees with the importance of cost reduction, quality workmanship, and similar manufacturing matters. To another observer, it may signify stress on economic enlightenment—on showing how investment creates jobs, or how high productivity is the road to high living standards. To a third party, substantial content may connote a leap by management into the arena of politics and partisan debate.

However one-track they may be, such recommendations are almost always dogmatic. What course is a company to select from the wide range of single-minded recipes for a publication worth the money it costs? "Which prophet am I to accept?" a plant manager once asked me.

To start, if management is realistic, it will be skeptical about all pat formulas for overnight success in any branch of employee relations or communications. It cannot afford to mistake a salesman's fervor for final truth.

Second—and most certainly in the field of employee publications—a management must cut its way through the jargon, the tangled surface details, and seek perspective. Turning away from talk of specific topics which might be included in its publication, it must first search for the basic principles involved. When such principles are discovered, the hitherto-confusing details generally fall into place, and management will have some kind of yardstick by which to decide what its publication should do and how it should do it.

Thus, at this point in the development of the employee publication, one need seems paramount: to codify some basic ground rules for establishing, guiding, and nourishing an effective periodical. Most desirably, such rules should have been tested by actual practice and be flexible enough to fit varied companies and a wide range of business problems.

To help fill that need by sharing one large company's experiences is the task set for this volume. Its goal is to enable managements, already publishing or about to do so, to realize a better return on their publication's dollars.

The conclusions described emerge from two types of experiences: (1) close study by the author and his associates of thousands of employee publications, plus discussions with hundreds of company editors and managements across the nation, and (2) the lessons learned during the establishment and growth of a diverse publications program within the author's own company. The Du Pont program includes 40 employee newspapers and magazines produced by plants in 21 states, and appearing at the rate of 800 issues a year; *Better Living*, a company-wide picture magazine for employees which has achieved considerable success; and numerous supervisory newsletters, stockholder bulletins, booklets, and special publications of the type common to nearly every business organization.

Such experiences always point to the uselessness of any "magic pill" formula which is pleasant tasting and guaranteed to solve all organizational ills. No detailed publications blueprint can be fitted over any and all enterprises, and no outsider can plan a company's publication program so well as its own people. Here, as in other realms, each enterprise's management, with an eye fixed on its own setting and peculiar problems, must do the ultimate design job itself. In doing so, however, it can profit from lessons learned in concentrated publications activity by other managements the nation over. To be of maximum value, of course, such lessons of experience should be formed into a body of guiding principles which all kinds of organizations can adapt in their publications planning.

At the outset, therefore, this book puts the employee periodical into perspective so that, as one manager urged, "we can tell the forest from the trees." Management's massive attempt to communicate *in writing* with employees is viewed as the symptom of a big change which has occurred in every phase of American life: the development of large organizations as the typical way by which the world's work gets done. A close look is taken at this change and at the salient characteristics and communications problems of organizations. I then discuss the function of a publication in such a setting; its advantages and disadvantages; the climate and conditions required for its successful use; and, finally, what experience shows a publication can and cannot do for its sponsors.

With this groundwork laid, the book passes on to a portfolio of actual house organ stories which displays the range and depth of subject matter the employee publication can treat. Finally, Part III relates the concrete steps a management can take to set up a new publication or improve the one it already has.

WILLIAM C. HALLEY

Acknowledgments

The authority for this book is the experience of the Du Pont Company and of the people who have been primarily concerned with its employee publications. The company's philosophy and practice are the essence of the point of view expressed, and the book blends the ideas of industrial management and editors who have contributed most to the Du Pont program. I should like, therefore, to acknowledge their role and express my thanks for their help in preparing this volume. In a handful of cases, I have specifically cited or reproduced their work; unfortunately, for each one singled out, there are dozens of others whose special insights and triumphs must go unheralded, though by no means forgotten.

As this book will emphasize repeatedly, no employee publications program can succeed without the strong and continuous support and encouragement of management. Du Pont management long ago recognized this need and provided the means for useful periodicals. Two men in particular grasped the possibilities and provided the leadership. One is Mr. Harold Brayman, Director of the Public Relations Department, whose vision and eloquent support of vigorous employee publications have pioneered fundamental improvements in management-employee communications, not only in Du Pont but also throughout industry. The second is Mr. Charles M. Hackett, Executive Assistant, Public Relations Department, whose original and fertile mind long ago foresaw and charted the editorial course that I think all worthwhile employee periodicals sooner or later are bound to take.

THE AUTHOR

Contents

Contents

PART III

EMPLOYEE PUBLICATIONS

Theory and Practice of Communications
in the Modern Organization

Part One

---

1. The Background

1. THE RISE OF EMPLOYEE PUBLICATIONS

The plant manager, a veteran of 25 years in industry, handed me the latest issue of his newspaper for employees. In it he had described the serious competitive problems the plant faced, reported plans for new investment and modernization, and detailed the steps each person could take to improve product quality.

"This newspaper's an interesting thing," he said. "When I was a foreman, we figured the employee publication had about as much future as the girls' softball team. It was pretty to look at and when it come out it attracted a lot of attention. But nobody thought it would come to this. In fact," he added, "if I were the only manager paying for a publication, I might worry about myself. But there are 30 local companies putting out these papers. Ten years ago, there weren't half a dozen."

The manager's surprise may well be shared by anyone whose career spans several decades. For in less than one man's business life, the employee publication has progressed from an organizational rarity to a standard feature of employee relations activities.

For example, in 1929, one authority estimates, the United States had 575 "house organs." Twenty years later, the number had grown to about 5,000, or 10 times as many, and, in the past decade, the number has doubled again to something on the order of 10,000.

Circulation of these periodicals has likewise zoomed. In 1952, *Fortune* estimated the total house-organ audience as approximately 100 million. Five years later, the International Council of Industrial Editors calculated, after careful study, that total coverage in this country and Canada reached an astonishing 300 million copies per issue—a figure double the total circulation of the top 120 magazines in the U.S. and Canada.

At the same time, total employment on the editorial side has climbed to between 12 and 15 thousand, while total annual budgets approach the $500 million mark. If employee publications should multiply as fast in the next 10 years as in the past decade, it is not at all unlikely that the total number of such periodicals will double, or even treble, by 1968, and that the editorial work force will begin to take on a dimension approaching that of the daily press itself.

The mounting importance of company publications is readily seen in the volume of press comment they inspire. *Fortune, Harvard Business Review, Time,* and a wide range of trade papers or management newsletters have repeatedly evaluated and advised the bantling press. In addition, the house organ has evoked a professional press of its own typified by *Stet,* The House Magazine for House Magazine Editors, and *The Editor's Notebook,* produced by the American Association of Industrial Editors. A market has even been found for catalogs listing several thousand publications as markets for free-lance writers.

The sheer magnitude of U.S. management's turn to the printed word rules out the possibility that company publications are the accidental offspring of high earnings or temporary fads. When 10,000 managements of all persuasions agree on any course of conduct, something fundamental is involved. In this case, a clue to the fundamental was suggested by an employee relations superintendent who observed, "Apparently we're not the only people who need large publications programs. Look at the unions, the churches, the Army."

For example, U.S. trade unions alone produce 650 weekly and 250 monthly publications with combined circulations in excess of 20 million, plus newsletters and other smaller periodicals. Religious bodies in this country publish some 1,000 magazines and newspapers. As for the Army, in addition to publications with such titles as *Troop Topics* and *Report to the Army*, the *Army Almanac* reports that "hundreds of small post, camp, and station newspapers are published today, from mimeographed sheets to large dailies."

That organizations with such widely differing purposes should venture so heavily into publications suggests that, to some degree, all large organizations share a common problem. To see this problem, it is necessary to examine in some detail the social changes which have caused organizational leaders to call upon the printed word.

2. THE RISE OF LARGE ORGANIZATIONS

The signal sociological phenomenon in America during the past century has been the rise of large organizations as the instruments by which human needs are served. This is true in nearly every field.

A hundred years ago, there were no labor unions, farm organizations, philanthropic foundations, or professional societies of any scale. Government was small, corporations were few, and large businesses were practically nonexistent. In 1849–50, the academic registration for Columbia University (present enrollment, circa 21,000) was a tiny 130 students.

Today, by contrast, every aspect of life is organized on a large scale. Some 94 labor unions, for example, have a membership of 25,000 or over. There are some 250 major U.S. religious bodies, with a combined total of more than 300,000 churches and 103 million members.

In education, although we have some 1,871 institutions of higher learning, the role assumed by the large university can also be seen in the fact that about 50 per cent of U.S. college enrollment is congregated in less than 8 per cent of the institutions.

The trend to large organizations can clearly be seen even in the daily press. Today, there are actually about 400 fewer daily newspapers than there were in 1900, yet total circulation is six times greater. A century ago, one could start a paper in New York City for about $15,000; today, the estimated requirement is five million dollars. By the same token, it takes an organization with capital of about one-half million dollars to equip a television station.

In agriculture, three major farm organizations enjoy combined memberships of nearly two million. In social service, there are more than 4,000 foundations or non-profit organizations. The American Red Cross boasts 20 million members and more than 3,700 chapters, while two million Americans belong to the YMCA. There are about 1,500 business trade associations; the American Legion maintains 17,000 local posts; while in government, one employee in eight of the nation's work force works for federal, state, or local agencies, compared with one worker in twenty-five only 50 years ago.

Even in science, long the domain of the lone wolf, an invention or development can rarely be attributed to an individual in the sense that the telephone is credited to Bell or the electric light to Edison. The scientific "team" is the standard pattern today.

In sum, what has been happening over the past century in every field has been the gradual replacement of individual effort by group effort on a scale never before known to man. The reason is simply that the large organization can perform feats and meet challenges that individuals working alone can never do.

The rise of large organizations and the change in the traditional role played by the individual are clearly evident in the panorama of business growth.

In the 250 years from the first colonies to mid-nineteenth century, U.S. business organizations were typically small, for agriculture was the primary industry. Markets were local and, therefore, limited; tools were crude; capital was scarce; and transportation was primitive.

By mid-nineteenth century, however, the Industrial Revolution had completed its jump across the Atlantic and was being exploited by native technologists and businessmen. To this trend, the Civil War gave a powerful stimulus. Between 1860 and 1870, the total number of U.S. manufacturing establishments increased by 80 per cent and the value of manufactured goods by 100 per cent. In the decades between Appomattox and the century's turn, the whole pattern of present industrial society was established, goaded by two powerful forces: (1) the pressures of a population which doubled in size between the end of the Civil War and 1900, and (2) the challenge of a vast, unexploited land empire of more than three million square miles,

nearly equal to Europe in size. In the regions beyond the Mississippi alone, the entire Roman Empire, glowingly described by the historian Gibbon, could be neatly tucked.

The large business organization became the effective instrument of the new economy, for the lone artisan or craftsman, the household industry, the small shop were not equipped to handle Herculean tasks. The mechanical revolution in industry, the operation of huge, integrated plants, the extension of railroads —all required large aggregations of capital and people. A dramatic indicator of the way the country was going came just after the turn of the century when the United States Steel Corporation was capitalized at $1,400,-000,000. This sum was larger than the total national wealth a century earlier.

The nineteenth century needs which fathered the large business organization continued to mount in the twentieth. Since 1900, population has again more than doubled and is still rising at a rate of nearly four million persons a year. Business organizations, like those in education, religion, and elsewhere, have kept pace. In 1904, only one company in the country had assets over $500 million; today, an organization labeled an "octopus" in Theodore Roosevelt's time is likely to be considered a smaller unit. For there are now 21 corporations with annual sales of $1 billion or more; 3,500 companies have more than 1,000 employees. Further, it has been estimated that, if the nation's future needs for goods are to be met, the number of businesses with more than 1,000 employees must double by 1976.

3. GROWTH BROUGHT HUMAN PROBLEMS

The benefits provided by large organizations in the fields of production, education, science, and philanthropy are well known.

In industry, for example, it was Andrew Carnegie himself who marveled to note that two pounds of ironstone, one and one half pounds of coal, one half pound of lime, and a small amount of manganese could be mined, transported to Pittsburgh, "and these four pounds of materials manufactured into one pound of steel, for which the consumer pays one cent."

The advantages bigness provides to the consumer are likewise evident in the case of today's automobile, which it has been estimated would cost $50,000 if manufactured in a backyard shop.

The very source of any organization's strength is the bringing together of large numbers of people and focusing their energies upon a single goal. But this raises a serious human question: how to maintain the identity and recognize the contribution of the individual in a world that increasingly must turn to the group or organization for progress.

A great deal has been said about the problems of the individual in adjusting himself to the organization. Grave fears are continuously expressed that the industrial worker or the student in a large university is a forgotten man, lost in the mesh of giant processes. We hear of robots and automatons, or of intellectual ciphers ground out by an educational assembly line.

Little has been said, however, about the other side of the coin—about the problems the organization itself faces in adjusting in an efficient and productive way to the myriad individual parts of which it is composed. This also is a crucial matter, because General Motors, the Baptist Church, and the American Medical Association alike have no life, talent, or capacity independent of their members. As any foreman can testify, the co-operation of individuals in an organization is voluntary and depends upon individual consent to serve group goals. This means that all successful leadership must seek to keep itself in spiritual and emotional harmony with the rank and file. Failure to do so leads at best to bureaucracy and dead-level mediocrity; at worst, it leads to extinction of the institution.

Keeping oneself in harmony with the individuals of an organization requires as an absolute minimum telling them what is going on. What are the organization's plans? What are its goals and the problems it must overcome in the coming year? Why are we doing what we're doing? Unless any organization attempts to keep its members posted on major topics, it is headed for eventual trouble.

It is obvious that publications are one part of a program by which an organization seeks to inform its people and to overcome communications problems posed by its physical scale. Such a program will also include a well-informed line organization: supervisors and foremen in industry, chancelors and deans in education, cardinals and bishops in churches. It may also include meetings, bulletins, letters, handbooks, motion pictures, bulletin boards, loud-speaker systems, and other channels.

Thus, before the particular role of the employee publication can be determined, it is important to examine in detail the obstacles an organization must overcome to keep its parts alive and dynamic. How can it keep individual incentives, performance, and morale at high levels? In industry specifically, what kinds of roadblocks does leadership face in solving this major management problem of the times?

2. Man and the Organization

1. AN OLD AMERICAN CONFLICT

A century ago, only one in four of the nation's breadwinners was an employee working for hire. The rest were independent enterprisers or artisans, farmers, or seasonal workers. Today, by contrast, four out of five of us earn wages or salaries as employed persons.

For better or worse, we are living in a corporate age, an age of groups, and we would not turn back if we could. And although this is true in nearly every realm of activity, there is little doubt that we still worship the memory of the freehold farmer of the past—the sturdy independent who worked his farm as he saw fit and hoed his row without consultation. To document this, one need not point to the henpecked husband who stoutly maintains the fiction that "I wear no man's collar!" A far more serious sign of this underlying conflict is seen in the peculiar mixture of admiration and fear with which Americans look upon the large organizations of their society.

This conflict is not new. In the height of Theodore Roosevelt's trust-busting days, the humorist Finley Peter Dunne ("Mr. Dooley") satirized the President's dilemma on big business thus: "Th' thrusts are heejous monsthers built up by th' inlightened intherprise ov th' men that have done so much to advance progress in our beloved counthry. On wan hand I wud stamp them undher fut; on th' other hand, not so fast."

Still today, we admire gigantic feats. When World War II evoked such production deeds as 106 Liberty ships in a single month, 100,000 aircraft in a single year, and steel production almost equal to the whole world's output in World War I, the nation was proud and grateful. Likewise, our breasts swell as we describe educational facilities which accommodate more than three million college students.

But at the same time, the large production organization and the teeming university are feared as evidence that the individual is no longer important. Most discussions range the individual on one side and the organization on the other as though the twain can never meet with satisfaction. Yet the fact is that an organization is no more than a collection of individuals, and the prime need of the present is to build awareness that coming together represents not smotheration, but implementation of individual talents and effort on a scale not otherwise possible.

2. DOES ANYONE KNOW I'M HERE?

Building such an understanding of our changed times is no overnight job. It is obvious that when any organization grows to the size of those which presently characterize our society, the scope of its activities easily overawes the individual who is its basic building block. "Who am I?," he inquires as he looks upward at the pyramid of the organization chart, senses complex processes at work, confronts swarms of people he will never know scurrying to unimaginable tasks. This feeling of personal isolation is deadly. If the individual lacks a proper understanding of the organization and the emotional conviction that he has a respectable and honorable place within it, the possibilities for personal estrangement and frustration are enormous.

It is for this reason that in all kinds of large organizations a carefully planned program to disseminate information is needed. Such a program will have two principal goals, the first of which is to enable the individual to *identify himself with the group to which he belongs*—a goal as important in business organizations as in churches, unions, and countries. The second goal of the program will be to *interpret to the individual the significance and value of his particular role and function within the group*. In effect, such an information program helps the individual to see himself in a new light in industry—not merely as a man holding down a job, but as a man engaged upon a work.

Once people are provided with such insight into their work, the results are often startling. During World War II, for example, workers at the Oak Ridge atomic materials plant, for security reasons, did not know what they were doing. "It has been reported that within one week after the bombing of Hiroshima, which dramatized to these workers what they were producing, production doubled. When the second bomb fell on Nagasaki, and further drove home to the workers the extent to which their efforts were hastening the end of the war, production quickly rose to 300 per cent of the original level."*

I noticed once a number of years ago that the owner of a small company with unusually harmonious labor relations always prefaced remarks to employees with an expression along these lines: "When you sit in my chair, the problem looks like this," and then he would explain his views on safety or waste or whatever.

This is a good technique and worked well in its setting. The worker does indeed need to see the plant as if he were its manager rather than a disaffected part. But creating this kind of feeling has become more and more difficult as even "small" organizations grow to more unwieldy proportions.

There can be no doubt that the root of "the communications problem" for any management is personal, physical dissociation from the work group. The large organization easily outgrows its nervous system and the head gets out of touch with the parts. Presidents of corporations have as little direct contact with the man in the chemical building as the Pope has with individual parishes or the leader of a large labor union has with local members. This fact is a source of potential trouble in any organization; if there is no joint understanding between top and bottom, joint purposes are impossible.

Earlier in our history, this was not a problem. In embryo industry, the owner hired "help." Owners like E. I. du Pont and their helpers were in close physical contact, meeting daily, it has been said, to chat over a dipper of water at the plant pump. Exchange of ideas, information, and opinion was easy and continuous; there existed the kind of employee relations situation which any thoughtful manager of today yearns for: a chance to meet employees face to face and to clear up misunderstanding and confusion at their sources.

When, for example, a Vermonter, Thaddeus Fairbanks, and his three brothers, began

---

* Herbert M. Baus, *Public Relations at Work*, p. 25, Harper & Brothers, New York, 1948.

to manufacture scales in the early nineteenth century, their shop was a wooden building 25 by 60 feet that was factory, warehouse, and salesroom combined. The company history reports that "The relationship which existed between the partners and their employees is indicated by an incident which occurred during the financial stringency in 1838. At that time, the workmen voluntarily signed and brought into the accounting room a paper suggesting their willingness to have monthly payments suspended until the company was in funds. Five months later, in February 1839, all back wages were paid."

In such a setting where owner and worker were persons well known to one another, opinions were not necessarily identical, but it was not difficult for "management" and "labor" to know where the other stood and the reasons for their attitudes. The employer's policies, sales efforts, and production problems were clear to all who had eyes to see. The employee's complaints, frustrations, and personal disturbances were exposed to light and did not seethe in secret.

Just as important to the employee's status as the direct transmission of news and opinion was the comparative ease with which the worker could identify his part in the effort of the whole. He was, obviously, an important member of the team; what his contribution was, all could see. More, his own eyes could roam over the whole enterprise. He knew the raw materials, the market, and the steps required to fabricate his product; he could generally take a craftsman's pride in his product's use by the consumers around him.

As departments, functions, and plants multiplied, however, quick and easy worker-identification with the enterprise became more difficult. Between owner and employee

yawned the ever-widening gulf of the organization chart. The A. O. Smith Corporation's history is typical: the company began life in 1874 to make parts for baby carriages. Twenty years later, its work force was multiplied many times and it was making bicycle frames. When the automobile came in at the century's turn, the company began to manufacture body frames, and its product lines and employee groups have steadily multiplied since that time.

Other important changes were wrought by the kind of business growth the U.S. has seen. Not only did it become impossible for "the owner" to know his employees intimately; in addition, management itself became more dispersed as firms became so large that they passed beyond the mental compass of a single proprietor. The vice president, someone humorously observed, was one of the primary inventions of the nineteenth century.

Ownership of a typical enterprise likewise spread and all organizational relationships took on an impersonal tone. Misunderstandings and hostilities naturally multiplied. Forty years after the Fairbanks incident reported above, the climate of industrial relations had markedly changed: the mammoth railroad strike of 1877, which idled 100,000 rail workers and spurred bloody battling in a dozen cities, was precipitated by a handful of employees protesting a reduction of wages necessitated by the nationwide business depression.

In addition to the increase in sheer numbers of people, a second factor making for individual "aloneness" was the vast, specialized technology which became characteristic of modern business. Mass production did not eliminate worker skills, but rather multiplied them; the percentage of unskilled people in the work force has been halved since 1910. Skills, however, have become somewhat rarefied; as in science, activities which were once single and whole have been split down into component atoms.

In the case of hourly or production workers, the effects of this development have been much commented upon. In fact, so often has it been said that the worker has trouble figuring out where he fits in that it is easy to forget that the human problems posed by specialization range far upward into the organization's ranks. A technical director told me that the title, Works Engineer, for example, once designated "the man who does the plant engineering work." Today, it designates an administrator under whom come as many as 70 or 80 different engineering specialties ranging from air-conditioning design to tiny aspects of process control. Without management effort to recognize and affirm the importance of such skills, the individual specialist might well feel himself to be a lost and forgotten cog.

It is commonly assumed, of course, that "professionals" and white-collar workers identify themselves with management and, therefore, do not need much special attention. This is a very dangerous assumption. The color of a man's collar no longer bestows the prestige it did in times past. White-collar activities have become so diverse and white-collar ranks so large that the term itself is a misnomer. Such workers comprise almost one fifth of the total work force today. In the past 10 years alone, it is estimated that office workers have increased nearly 50 per cent. As this trend develops in the future, it seems likely that the hallowed white collar will shed much of its power as a symbol of achievement and badge of management rank.

In fact, this vast and growing middle-ground of business is in danger of becoming a floating population not identified either with management or labor. That unions have had meager success to date in organizing white collars is not a sign that such workers identify themselves with management and the direction of the enterprise. Rather, it probably means that they do not consider themselves "labor," as indicated by the changing appeals with which unions approach this group. Most likely, the eventual penalty for taking the white-collar worker for granted is not unionization, but inefficiency, characterized by corrosive personal frustration. I once shared a car pool with an accounting supervisor who was an extreme example of what can happen when organizational "backwaters" are allowed to develop. Although his was a fairly responsible job, management was always "they"; he cursed the houses of management and labor alike and vaguely suspected that even his retirement party was some kind of hypocritical fraud. A sick man, perhaps, but, unless precautions are taken, his disease might easily become epidemic.

To construct a program designed to compensate for the revolutionary changes in the work setting and in management-employee relationships, the first step is to determine what kind of situation would be ideal, both for organization and for the individual. What kind of condition do we wish to restore? What should the individual be expected to give to the organization, and what should he logically desire to receive in return?

3. ORGANIZATION TAKE AND GIVE

The organization that will be highly successful must seek something more from the individual than that passive state summed up by the expression "job satisfaction." Moderate energies and nodding acquiescence of employees will not make any organization effectual in reaching its goals.

The enterprise must really seek what has been aptly called willing dedication. As one reflective manager put it, "Ideally, I would like each man to do his job feeling that he has a personal responsibility for the results we get as a company."

This kind of employee-identification, obviously, is not easily won, nor, once won, retained forever. Most important, it is not a gift. The enthusiastic, hard-driving, and creative employee at every level approaches his job in that manner because he gets something more than money in return for his contribution.

His extra reward is satisfaction of the emotional need to be treated as a whole man rather than merely a hand. The take-home pay of the responsible employee includes what the experienced foreman capsules as "recognition"—not the kind of scattergun recognition which comes with having one's name listed in the telephone book, but the kind of singling out which focuses on a man's responsibilities and skills, which conveys to him and to the world that he is a successful human being.

This means that the employee needs evidence that the organization respects him as a person to whom fair and consistent treatment is due. He expects recognition that he is not a machine attachment, but a dignified individual doing work which is meaningful and serious, and regarded so by the organization.

Twenty-five years ago, in a series of pioneering personnel studies, Western Electric Company found that any change in working conditions, even for the worse, resulted in higher productivity by a selected group of girls. The key factor motivating high performance was not job conditions or work load, but management's obvious interest in, and concern for, the persons of the group. They were singled out for attention.

This finding is still valid. The desire for personal status, natural to all men, extends far upward into an organization. A recent study by Opinion Research Corporation of supervision in 43 companies concluded that a prime motivation of the foreman is pride in the symbols of personal achievement that come with being recognized as a leader of men. "What the supervisor's ego craves is assurance from management that he is wanted, needed, valued in the corporate scheme. Such things, in fact, should be ceremonialized in the form of dinners, awards, regular meetings with higher management sitting in, and perquisites."

These unexpressed emotional demands of an organization's people must be satisfied in some way. If the individual feels himself to be forgotten and his personal efforts futile and unappreciated, the organization is not going to get his best efforts; much more likely, it is going to suffer severely from a boiling hostility which has no apparent cause.

A foreman recently provided an interesting case history. Under him was an excellent long-service operator—a little reticent perhaps, but, if ever there was a satisfied employee, Red was the man.

Then came the day when the plant's first Open House was scheduled. At each major point along the process, someone was designated to explain the operation to the visiting families. Red wasn't selected, and suddenly the quiet man exploded in a highly illuminating way. He had worked these dryers for 12 years, he said; he had practically put them in. He knew more about them than the operators, the foreman, and the company president put together. He had the best quality and attendance record in the department. But when an Open House came along, was he chosen as a speaker? No. *After twenty years, he said, no one even knew he was around the place.*

In the ensuing conversation, the foreman found out two major things about Red. First, the operator was convinced that nobody cared anything about him; all "they" wanted was for him to do his job and not to bother anybody. Second, the foreman found, Red had only the foggiest notions about his plant's process and people. He was not clear on operations one step removed from his own; he had not yet heard of two new, major product applications; he did not know what "the construction people" were doing on the site, although he had seen the cranes and some people wearing hard hats. As for the methods engineers who had transformed his area for the better—they were "speed-up" men; management was "those guys in the front office." In fact, Red's entire fund of information was a blend of rumors, partial facts, and speculation.

Whose fault was it? Nobody's actually, the foreman said. For when he checked his other peoples' opinions over the next few weeks, he found that, to some extent, all showed traces of Red's feeling of futility. The only "villain" was a large and complex organization.

It is to compensate for this kind of problem that the employee periodical can render maximum service to management. When it is no longer possible for leadership of an organization physically to meet people, the publication can serve as an artificial, but highly effective, substitute. It enables a manager to insure that his people are kept informed, that they are experts who understand the meaning of the work they do, the process they operate, and the product they make. Through a paper also, the manager can interpret policy and practices, cite personal skills and workmanship, applaud quality records and other personal achievements, and generally do in writing what he is no longer able to do in person.

No publication, of course, will be complete and entire of itself. Almost by definition, a first-rate information program depends upon a well-trained and indoctrinated supervisory force; it is through the supervisor that top management can make flesh-and-blood contact with people.

In smaller organizations, it sometimes happens that supervision is the only channel needed. In most cases, though, the "management representative" will need auxiliary aids. For a program that depends upon passing along information by word of mouth has two prime pitfalls: first, as organization lines become longer and way stations along the route from top to bottom become more numerous, accurate transmission of authoritative information is difficult. The prevalence of rumor, grapevine, and scuttlebutt testify that a management statement is altered, edited, and revised by each link in the communications chain. A set of facts which leaves the front office clear and understandable may be barely recognizable by the time it reaches the men in the river pump house.

Second, a program of information based solely on verbal transmission must assume that the foreman is blessed with funds of information which not even a manager would profess. It is often glossed over that a working supervisor's primary concern is the physical functioning of his group, its schedule of jobs, its safety, and its harmony. The 8-hour day alone precludes his dwelling for long upon topics which do not bear directly upon the job immediately at hand.

Thus, it is to provide a direct line from management to every corner of the organization that the arts of journalism have found their way into the business and industrial scene.

Long before they concern themselves with the techniques of actual publications production, most managers declare it essential to determine basic policy carefully. Without a backbone of firm principle to guide a venture into print, management's judgment is likely to be swamped by a sea of details; the publication in such cases follows a freakish course, changing tack as the wind blows and the latest management convention recommends.

A first step, therefore, is to take a realistic look at publication purposes and to decide exactly why organizations spend money on the written word. It is also important to be aware of publication pitfalls, strengths, and weaknesses. These matters are discussed in following chapters.

3. The Process of Persuasion

1. THE PUBLICATION'S PRIME JOB

Some years ago, I sat on a panel with the editor of a lavish magazine produced by a large company. The publication was new, ambitious, and, because of its handsome appearance, had several times been cited for "excellence" by the agencies which do such things. It was, therefore, with some astonishment that I heard him tell the audience of mingled editors and employee relations managers that "we don't really have any specific goals. We just try to do a good job."

It is not easy to see how one can do the second in the absence of the first. "Why are we planning to publish?" should be the first question a management asks itself, and it should seek answers which can be stated clearly and concisely.

I suspect my friend either of being excessively modest or of not telling all he knew. For it is a fact that business people are frequently embarrassed to say realistically and forthrightly what they would like a publication to do.

Obviously, the first job of any worth-while organizational publication is consciously to promote the well-being of the organization that pays for it. Nearly always this means that its function is to persuade others to support a point of view, to admit new facts to the mind, or to adopt a desired course of conduct.

This is usually clear to institutions like churches or schools, or to individuals like politicians or union leaders. But although business organizations are as dependent as any other group upon the loyalty and support of their members, they frequently feel that "persuasion" smacks of "propaganda." Propaganda is a dirty word, reminiscent of Joseph Goebbels and Nazi Germany, of political demagoguery.

In actual fact, the word "propaganda" had an honorable birth in the early 1600's, when the Roman Catholic Church, under Pope Gregory XIII, established a committee for the "propagation of the faith." The object was to win converts and persuade mankind of the truths of church doctrine.

But long before propaganda had a name, it was at work in every aspect of social life. No man with anything on his mind can open his mouth without thereby seeking in some sense to persuade others. It is difficult to think of a single classic work of philosophy, literature, oratory, history, or art which is not a moving expression of ideas and beliefs for which the author sought acceptance. Variously urging men to some vision of the good life were Jeremiah the Hebrew, Plato the Greek, and Augustine the Christian. The poet Virgil sought to justify Rome's right to rule the world, while Kipling glorified the British Empire. Julius Caesar's *Gallic Wars*, like *The Federalist Papers* of Hamilton, Madison, and Jay, were appeals to the public for political support.

By the same token, any well-conceived organizational publication consciously seeks to move to some desired action a group within our society. This is true of a college alumni magazine like *Harvard Today*, a religious periodical like *The Watchtower* of the Jehovah's Witnesses, and a professional organ like the *Journal of the American Medical Association*. It is equally true also of an employee periodical produced by a business organization.

Obviously, "persuasion" may be bad as well as good. All depends upon the program's object, method, and content. It is "bad" if its purpose is to distort the truth or subjugate nations, à la Moscow, or if it advances irresponsible movements like Townsend's $200-a-month-to-be-spent-before-payday.

On the other hand, persuasion is good and honorable if it tells the truth and if its purpose is constructive: to raise funds for a boys' club, or to win support for cancer research or to promote the success of a socially valuable cause or institution.

Like church prelates and university presidents, business managers can be advocates without being rogues.

2. THE UNDERLYING PURPOSES

The specific themes an organizational publication will attempt to register with its readers will vary tremendously—with the institution, the times, and the organization's immediate and future problems. For this reason, a quick glance at a given issue of a periodical is more likely to confuse than reveal the underlying purpose. For example, articles in a given issue of an industrial newspaper may be urging the employee to avoid injury, or to accept personal responsibility for good workmanship, or to understand the role of new investment in building plant and employee security.

Underneath the seeming variety of a well-conceived periodical, however, there are two dominant purposes. The first is to help the individual identify himself with the organization and to take pride in its achievements. The validity of this principle is clearly shown in military groups like the U.S. Marine Corps; the individual's pride in belonging to a famous organization with high standards and notable traditions is one of the Corps' most potent weapons. Man indeed does not live by bread alone; in industry, religion, or education, the organization is in trouble if the individual does not point proudly to "my plant," "my church," and "my college."

The second function of a publication then becomes that of winning members' support for the organization's goals and objectives. It attempts to keep the organization healthy and vigorous by reporting its needs and problems and by pointing out what the individual can do to help. In industry, the employee may be encouraged to participate in a cost-reduction program designed to improve the plant's competitive position; on an overseas army base, the troop paper may urge soldiers to fraternize amicably with the natives; in education, an alumni bulletin may call for financial aid to compensate for inflation's impact on the institution's endowment.

3. PREREQUISITES FOR PERSUASION

Once a business management decides upon its publication's purpose, it can then profitably consider the conditions which must prevail before a newspaper or magazine can do its job with maximum efficiency.

The first and most important of these conditions is a management-employee climate of mutual trust and respect. Many employee relations problems have their origins in misinformation or in businessmen's traditional reluctance to take employees into confidence. But a sudden management switch to the vocal will not automatically repair the damage wrought by past silence. Ignorance may have created hostile attitudes which now have a life of their own and act as major roadblocks to harmony. An audience convinced that its interests run counter to those espoused by a publication will usually ignore, discount, or resist the most compelling array of facts. If the reverse is true, and the climate is one of mutual confidence, there is a good chance that what the publication says will be received favorably and that co-operation will be forthcoming.

A clear-cut example of these principles is provided by the attempts of the British to raise output in the coal-mining industry. The industrial psychologist, T. M. Higham, reporting a study by the Acton Society Trust (1952), wrote that every attempt was made to tell the miners why a higher output was necessary. "Pamphlets, magazines, even a personal letter from the then Prime Minister, Mr. Attlee, were employed." But the mere provision of information did not reduce proneness to prejudice, nor did it succeed in modifying the underlying attitude of mistrust.

Higham concludes: "It seems clear that to insure good reception, you must create the right atmosphere. This is, perhaps, the one prerequisite for effective communication. Where it does not exist, communication will be difficult and what is said is likely to be distorted."

A climate of confidence, of course, depends heavily upon whether or not the "audience" believes the speaker to be credible. This in turn depends upon whether it thinks him to be trustworthy, expert and, most important, upon whether or not he appears to be furthering ulterior motives.

A remarkable nonindustrial instance of audience reaction to a credible speaker is Kate Smith's War Bond Radio Marathon of 1943. In a 16-hour period, the singer broadcast 65 impassioned appeals; the response was a fantastic total of $39 million worth of bond pledges. When a sample of her radio listeners was interviewed by trained psychologists and sociologists, it was found that the link uniting all auditors was belief in Kate Smith's integrity. They were not personally acquainted with her, may never have seen her, knew her only as a disembodied voice. But they believed she was real, genuine, and sincere. When she asked them to buy bonds, they were moved to do so.

Fortunately, there is considerable evidence that management in general is considered a highly credible source of information by employees. An Opinion Research Corporation study made as early as 1947, when most employee publications were in infancy, found that "in the main, employees do believe what their publication tells them." In the cases of five companies representing steel, oil, electrical equipment, and chemical industries, as high as 91 per cent of employees in individual instances felt that their publication was truthful. One publication scored only 64 per cent, which led the study to conclude that the employee publication "is part of the whole complex the employee calls 'the company.' This being the case, employee reaction is the result not only of what is on the printed page, but also of the spirit of management's relationships with the rank and file."

In sum, a high credibility source is an individual or institution with a reputation for integrity and truthfulness. A good reputation is easy to lose if deeds suggest that peoples' confidence is misplaced. The reverse is likewise true: a bad reputation is hard to dispel. And this is undoubtedly why even the most sincere attempts to improve practices and policies frequently meet employee suspicion. People bring to any situation a mental set and attitudes which they have previously learned; new proposals, plans and friendly overtures must overcome the lessons of the past. In this respect, perhaps, the adage, "Once burned, twice shy," may be considered a law of industrial life.

4. KNOWING THE AUDIENCE

Any organization embarking upon a program of persuasion must possess detailed knowledge of the audience to which it is talking. True, within a given club, church, or industrial plant, members will share common interests. But within any organization will also be found extreme variations in intellectual ability, occupation, and personal outlook.

In industry, for example, the audience for a typical company publication may include people in research, engineering, and sales as well as clerks and production workers. A single publication of equal interest and pertinence to all is impossible; the more heterogeneous the audience, the more diffused the material in a publication must be, and the greater the likelihood of failure. In trying to please all, the publication pleases none.

This internal problem is further complicated when the publication doubles in brass as an "external," which about 14 per cent of company periodicals attempt to do. Such a periodical seeks to appeal not only to employees, but also to the public—and, in particular, customers. The dilemma is obvious. An external's job is to sell goods to customers; such readers will exhibit scant interest in features designed to show that the company's employee benefit plans are liberal. Likewise, the employee's interests and needs are usually quite different from those of customers. The

editor is somewhat in the position of a man having to make a successful speech to an audience composed equally of Democrats and Republicans.

The ideal solution is to direct a separate publication to each of the audiences. If this is impossible, the only sensible alternative is to pick out the majority group—the one management believes to be the most important—and beam the publication at it.

In industry, particularly on a single plant location, the majority audience will generally be the large body of production operators and mechanics. Most persuasive and educational efforts by management will, therefore, be directed at this group. Problems arise when a plant location also includes a laboratory or technical installation employing people who are above average in education and/or sophistication. Such a group is apt to express indifference to a publication beamed at the man in the plant. They may at times protest as forcefully as did one scientist in a chemical plant who affirmed that the plant newspaper was edited "by idiots for idiots." What the chemist felt people really wanted was "technical discussions and reports on research studies."

The chemist was wrong. In such cases, a management can only grit its teeth and focus upon the larger audience, or it can emulate the managing editor of a large engineering and construction organization: two thirds of his audience was technically trained people. The publication goal for them was to build pride in their scientific knowledge and important technical achievements.

However, the editor also served a large home office force of clerical workers, plus construction sites where every kind of craftsman and manual worker was represented. The goal for this audience was quite different from that for technical people. Eventually, it was concluded that the only solution was two periodicals: (1) a professional journal for technical personnel and (2) a newspaper whose focus was largely upon the other groups.

Not every organization will be composed of such heterogeneous audiences as those cited. But in every case, the paramount matter which must be decided before a publication is planned in detail is "Who is the audience we want to talk to?"

5. KNOW WHO'S DRIVING

The importance of identifying the publication's audience and its special needs, however, should never obscure another basic point: it is not the reader but organizational leadership which drives the publication and decides upon its content. If this is not so, the periodical is not an instrument of persuasion at all, but an entertainment comparable to the employee recreation program.

In the abstract, this point seems rather obvious; in concrete, day-to-day production of employee publications, few principles are easier to forget. Often, in fact, it can be said that a prime disease of management publications is an obsessive concern with reader likes and dislikes.

Many miscalculations on this score probably stem from the popularity of catch phrases like "communications is a two-way street." If such an expression means that management should know what the organizational audience thinks and believes, it is undeniably true. Leadership must seek constantly to find out just how much information employees possess and upon what subjects they are uninformed. But no publication can be a two-way street any more than loud speakers, bulletin boards, or motion pictures

can be. A periodical is a one-way street from management to employees. And the preferences expressed by employees cannot be permitted to divert management from presenting the kind of serious discussion that it knows is in the best interests of the organization.

Yet it is not uncommon to see industrial managements and editors hopefully circularizing their subscribers to see what features pleased them most, and even asking their advice and counsel on what editorial matter would be most to their liking. Quite typical are the following three questions taken at random from a reader survey conducted by a large concern in the South:

"Do you think our company newspaper should help you to learn more about the company?"
"What kinds of stories would you like to see in the newspaper?"
"Do you find stories about the company and business interesting? Should they be continued?"

This kind of query, repeated thousands of times annually, dilutes any publication's effectiveness, for it takes the wrong stance. The real task of the employee periodical is not so much to give employees what they like, but rather to make them like what they need.

Clearly, the situation might be different if management's viewpoint and problems were widely understood and appreciated—if organizational harmony did not suffer because of misconceptions, distortions, and hostility. In such a state, there would be no need for management comment, interpretation, and explanation, and likewise no need for employee publications.

But mammoth problems, vitally connected

to the health of business institutions, do exist. Inside industry, there is the constant internecine struggle symbolized by labor quarrels. Even in the war years, the 1941–45 average of man-days lost to strikes was more than 36,000,000. Between 1950 and 1956, the average exceeded 30,000,000 annually, with a range all the way from 22,000,000 man-days to 59,000,000.

Equally serious problems come from without, either in the form of direct political assault or as dangerous, inaccurate ideas entertained by the public about business. In studies of public attitudes toward "big business," for example, the following notions repeatedly appear: big business crowds out small business; it is monopolistic and has no effective competition; it sets prices too high; it is greedy and its profits are too large; it concentrates too much power and exerts too much influence in government. On the human side, business is likewise scored: it is said to have no concern for, or interest in, people; the wage worker is nameless and faceless; the middle ranks of business are drowned in a sea of conformity; the business leader himself is ruthless, grasping, and scheming for personal power. Similar misconceptions and caricatures are continuously nurtured in television plays, novels, political oratory, and even comic books.

Such problems will not magically disappear of themselves; certainly the ominous public misconceptions of business life and practice will not be dispelled by any effort of the businessman's assailants. Management will have to correct the record itself.

And the advocate, whether his cause be a business institution, a political doctrine, or a spiritual outlook, cannot shape his sentiments to the pleasure of his public. Rather, he must use all his skills and talents to advance his views no matter how indifferent, apathetic, or hostile his publics may seem. No management can profitably abandon its educational objectives because queried employees say they would prefer cheesecake to a discussion of depreciation and obsolescence. It must manage its publication as it manages production, sales, and other aspects of the business.

4. Prime Pitfalls of Persuasion

1. GOALS THAT ARE TOO NARROW

For many years, a large plant had published an employee newspaper which had no discernible value. It contained the usual joke columns, shift personals, want ads and pictures made at the annual picnic, but little which could be called serious. Then one day, a cost-reduction program came along; a hard look was taken at every activity, and, under such scrutiny, the plant publication staggered. Obviously, it did little to justify itself.

"We have only ourselves to blame for that," the Personnel Superintendent told the manager's staff. "We staff members never try to decide what the paper should say; at best, we stress what it should *not* say. Naturally, when it comes out we can't see that it's doing much for the plant."

Accordingly, it was decided to revamp the publication from the ground up, and to use it to "advance the interests of this organization." But that simple, clean decision opened up a question which really requires some concentrated mental effort. Just how do you advance the interests of an organization? What kind of goals do you set? What subjects does your publication discuss? How does it discuss them? What should be avoided?

It is at this stage of management cogitation, I think, that the best-intentioned program of persuasion can get off the track, usually in one of two ways: first, the organization may set program objectives which are too narrow, self-serving, and exclusive; or second, it may do the reverse and venture into areas far beyond its legitimate sphere of interest.

The first pitfall, that of ostrich-like goals, is largely the result of taking too limited a view of what constitutes the organization's self-interest. Seemingly based on the philosophy of "every man for himself," such a program seeks to promote a particular organization as though it were the only one in the world. The fate of similar organizations is presumably their lookout.

Such attitudes are not novel, by any means. Under the Articles of Confederation, the infant American republic was well-nigh destroyed so violently did the states seek to magnify their separate interests at the expense of united action.

And frequently such attitudes can be described in miniature even within a single company. It is not uncommon to find a plant management emphasizing that "our only concern is this unit"—whereupon it proceeds to ignore the larger problems and issues which it decides are the exclusive property of "the company." It is true that a specific process-yield or cost-reduction problem rates top billing among a local unit's concerns. But it is clear also that any single plant will share the fate of its company as a whole. If a firm is exorbitantly taxed or weakened by hostile public opinion, a given unit will not escape unscathed though its cost-reduction program be the finest in the world.

The same is true on the broader canvas. No company or business is an island; it will share the fate of the business community. The major perils to churches, universities, or businesses alike come to them as institutions, not as individuals. The very currency of an expression like "big business" is evidence that our most sweeping pronouncements, good or bad, are upon the over-all pattern rather than upon individual companies. No particular merits it possesses, for example, would exempt any firm from a profits tax of 60 per cent, or 70, or 80, if such legislation were decreed. Whether or not it paid would be determined by its "bracket."

This means that, in any program of information, a company should consciously seek to interpret not just itself, but business generally. When a publication discusses business size or profits or technology, it should actually be presenting a case history of a much larger story—that of the competitive enterprise system itself. Otherwise the educational job is only half done.

2. GOALS THAT ARE TOO BROAD

A second, more obvious pitfall of persuasion is setting sweeping publication objectives which take management into areas of the employee's personal life that might well be none of the organization's business. The relationship between any organization's goals and the personal prerogatives of the individuals within the group is one of the most delicate balances in nature, and one of the most explosive. History suggests that when any organization extends its sphere of influence so that it begins to intrude into personal lives, the result is usually disastrous. To cite the political realm, it might be said that revolutions, American, French, or Russian, sprang from insupportable pressure and arrogant leadership. In America's case, it is interesting to note that a prime trigger of rebellion was a series of acts appropriately labeled "Intol-

erable." Similarly, the Protestant Reformation was in large part rejection of church primacy in all aspects of life.

Thus, any program of persuasion must avoid giving the impression that it is concerning itself with matters which are not its proper domain. It will, therefore, be helpful at this point to examine in some detail the relationship between individual and organizational goals, together with some of the areas in which management publications must tread with caution.

To begin with, there can be little doubt that membership in an organization does indeed exact from the individual certain abridgments of personal inclination and behavior. "Individuals entering into society must give up a share of liberty to preserve the rest," the Constitutional Convention concluded in 1787. Taking a wife and becoming a family man involves major modifications of the personal freedom of bachelorhood. Man the Homeowner must adjust himself to the mores and architectural tastes of his neighbors. Man the Political Animal must pay taxes to government. Man the Auto Owner must obey the speed limit. The list is endless, for all organized activity imposes standards of conduct.

A business organization sets up the individual's job conditions and his hours of work. It requires daily attendance, discourages malingering and exacts obedience to the instructions of supervision. It insists that the individual concentrate upon his task throughout the work day. If safety regulations require that the individual divest himself of a wrist watch or ring which might be caught in moving machinery, he must accept the organization's mandate. If the organization feels that a peccadillo like chin whiskers compromises a salesman's functioning as a company representative, it can with perfect sense hand him a razor.

In sum, the organization can with justice demand as its due from the employment contract individual deportment, habits, and conduct which it feels are essential to the enterprise's success. Any organization—university, labor union, or medical society—makes demands upon the individual.

By the same token, however, the individual preserves certain personal domains inviolate. As a free man, he enjoys inalienable personal rights; to transgress them is to be guilty of intrusion. He may elect to be a Mason, a materialist, or a devil worshipper. He may think what he likes, live where he pleases, and drive the car he prefers. To attempt to dictate on any such subject digs a grave for any program of persuasion; it will create resentment which alienates the individual and colors his every relationship with the organization. No irritated reader is likely to identify himself with the objectives of a company which is eternally sticking its nose into his private affairs and paternally telling him what to do and what to think.

3. POLITICS—YES OR NO?

A case in point is politics. One of the warmest discussions yet inspired by employee publications has revolved about this question: should a management periodical discuss political subjects with employees, or should it shun such fare?

Historically, such matter has been labeled "too controversial" and frequently ruled off limits by management. Spokesmen for this point of view still exist in large numbers and eloquently urge that attempts to present management's views on political questions is a violation of individual privacy. In its extreme form, this viewpoint was summed up by one editor thus: "It does not seem to be fully realized that the employee publication enters the employee's home as a guest—in most cases, an uninvited one. No guest would be so presumptuous as to lecture his host on the merits of his company, what's wrong with unions or right with them, the ethics of the profit motive, why he should participate in civic activity, or vote Republican, or any other matter related to the host's private life and views."

Therefore, by this view, the employee periodical should stick to innocuous fare, not only in political matters, but in practically all areas of serious concern to organizational leadership.

Increasingly in recent years, however, the spotlight has focused upon a diametrically opposed opinion. This insists that unless management speaks up on every political subject, it will be crushed in the war of ideas. It holds that of all the forces and agencies which appeal for the employee's loyalty—unions, political leaders, and pressure groups—only management fails to compete seriously. It thereby risks destruction by basking in the notion that an employee periodical should treat its readers like intellectual lightweights.

Where treatment of political subjects is concerned, many management spokesmen point with dismay to the heavy political content of union publications. In one influential article in the *Harvard Business Review*, for example, Fred W. Foy, President of the Koppers Company, and Robert W. Harper likened management to a fighter going into the ring with one hand tied behind his back in "its battle with the unions to win employee support for the American economic system."

In a study of the economic and legislative goals of unions, the authors documented in detail the efforts of union periodicals to implement these goals, most often in the form of recommended legislation. These ranged from calls for "positive action under the Full Employment Act of 1946" to "statements of the union's case for increased government intervention in the power industry" to tax relief to criticism of the Eisenhower Administration's foreign policy and many other matters.

"Unfortunately, we cannot provide actual examples of what management did to balance the union on the four subjects of unemployment, taxes, public power, and the Eisenhower Administration. We just did not find any, in our whole search of 700 company magazines," the authors reported, calling for an all-out business campaign to match union efforts to persuade.

The two points of view expressed here are the extremes, and it seems likely that the best course for most companies will be somewhere in between.

Obviously, politics and political questions cannot be ignored. Americans decide by the vote what is socially useful and worthy of encouragement and continuance, and the ultimate fate of business or any other institution will be decided at the polls. Thus it is not realistic for any management to assume that business alone of all groups in our society should express no views or preferences on political matters. In that direction lies the grave.

Most managements would decide, however, that they should no more go overboard on discussion of political issues than upon any other subject. Politically speaking, the most reasonable fare for the employee periodical would be issues which deal strictly with the success or health of business organizations. Few persons would deny that a management is justified in presenting a factual, well-rea-

soned case on a topic such as taxation; few would dispute the wisdom of documenting taxation's impact on the enterprise or its expansion plans or its incentive. Like a university or church, a business organization has a perfect right to speak when its existence or health are threatened.

On the other hand, it is by no means certain that a business organization should undertake to attack or espouse any political party, platform, or personality, if only because it must survive no matter who is in the White House. And partisan politics is as far outside its legitimate sphere as vegetarianism; certainly such topics as U.S. foreign relations are rather far removed from the business of running a plant successfully.

Thus, the line between legitimate and questionable political fare—admittedly a fine one —would isolate for treatment in the employee periodical only those subjects which are pertinent to the organization's successful operation, and can readily be recognized as such by the employee.

When it ranges too far afield, the employee publication may be antagonizing more readers than it persuades, or making itself ridiculous by asking employees to take sides on issues which do not concern them or about which they can do little.

Attempts to persuade on irrelevant, nonindustrial topics easily begin to sound like intrusion and spur the kind of exasperation and suspicion that renders the employee unreceptive on matters of much greater importance to all parties concerned.

4. THE TONE OF VOICE

I have said earlier that an employee publication is an attempt to restore as best management can the situation that prevailed when the owner and worker could meet at day's end to discuss affairs over a dipper of water at the pump. Obviously, a perfect substitute has not been devised if management makes its points by figuratively banging the employee on the head with the dipper.

This brings up the third major pitfall to any program of persuasion: the tone of voice with which it is conducted. It is possible, of course, that a publication will deliver a message so delicately that the reader cannot quite decide what it is driving at. Much more likely, however (and particularly when the subject is one on which management holds strong convictions), is a publication tone so forceful and domineering that it instantaneously antagonizes the reader.

It is easy to go awry, especially when smarting under a particularly outrageous charge or perverse bit of misinformation. A civic dignitary asserts that plant wastes are killing all the fish in the creek, or the union announces that it should appoint half the foremen—in such cases, the native human impulse is to strike back or to adopt a heavily ironic air of it's-time-somebody-straightened-you-out, friend.

But I can imagine no circumstance in which it is wise for a management publication to lose its patience. The truth, delivered in an offensive or provocative way, makes no headway at all. No organization can coerce agreement; it must seek consent. Sarcasm, a tone of outrage or invective seldom persuade anyone except those who are already on one's side; with others, such techniques may merely unite opposition. As any boy with a black eye knows, it is scant satisfaction merely to give as good as one gets.

In addition to avoiding quarrels and emotional debates, an effective publication will never stir up antagonisms by directly assail-

ing beliefs, causes, or organizations with which the individual associates himself. To imply that a man's wife or church or lodge or political party is undesirable constitutes a personal affront as surely as flinging down the gauntlet. More, when any man is challenged directly upon his opinions or affiliations, he is backed into a corner and forced to defend them—to take sides against the attacker. When his personal esteem is threatened, he squares off to fight instead of agreeing that he should change his mind.

5. THE MATTER OF DIGNITY

Many of the preceding matters may be summarized by saying that, at all times, an employee publication must keep its dignity and observe the proprieties of courteous conduct. It is not that organizational leadership can ever be "too proud to fight." Maintaining dignity even when provoked is, in this case, a strategical matter of not fighting upon an antagonist's terms—on his choice of ground and by a method he would welcome.

Leadership in any organization must stand for something solid, honest, and responsible. It cannot profitably descend to the level of petty argument or sniping debate, and it cannot win supporters by trying to shame them in print.

However, to say that management should not take up a publication like a cudgel does not mean that any topic likely to have an emotional charge is *verboten*. Far from it. Management publications were born because serious differences of opinion and outlook exist and are multiplying. But realistic planning in any form of persuasion demands that subjects be dealt with so that they enlighten rather than infuriate. And this means that the employee publication can never take its emotional tone, its style, and its manner from its competitors. It must steer an unswerving course of reason, logic and fact—issue after issue and year after year.

To persuade, management must, in Washington's words, "raise a standard to which the wise and honest can repair." This is the most promising formula for long-term success.

5. The Techniques of Persuasion

1. THE ROLE OF REPETITION

The worker at any level of a business enterprise spends approximately one third of his adult life in the work situation. He is understandably interested in knowing more about the people, activities, processes, and organization around him. Thus, the plant or company publication usually has great intrinsic appeal—more, perhaps, than any other kind of serious printed matter except the small-town newspaper.

It does not necessarily follow that the employee's interest in his publication insures that one presentation of one idea is sufficient to register it. The significance of management's message may be missed or passed over entirely. Sometimes the reason is purely physical: the mailman may inadvertently have failed to deliver the issue, or the employee may have come home tired and forgotten all about the paper.

But even more likely in the case of a serious business publication, a given article may fail to make contact because the ideas it advances are complex or require a good deal of mental effort by the reader.

For this reason, the employee periodical must take extra precautions to insure that important information gets through. This demands conscious adoption of techniques which are part of all educational and persuasive effort.

Without any question, the most important of these procedures is *repetition*. Human beings do not absorb facts or ideas quickly.

The necessity for repetition is evident to any parent who has tried to teach a child a poem, or to any minister who rises each week to remind his congregation of its religious principles. It is likewise evident to people in safety and accident-prevention programs, as suggested by the National Safety Council's annual output of some 10,000,000 posters.

Similarly, almost all managements stress the importance of repetition in such activities as sales or advertising. Customers are called upon frequently and systematically; radio or television programs and striking magazine and newspaper ads work constantly to establish a company's name and products with consumers. When it comes to selling its ideological wares over and over, however, many managements have seemed to shy away from this necessary step.

I recall a plant manager once telling me that he hoped he had seen the last of newspaper features describing to employees the meaning of "return on investment."* "Ye Gods," he said, "how many times do you think you have to tell people the same thing?" Interestingly enough, a few minutes later the manager called a meeting to devise a cost-reduction slogan to be broadcast to employees for the next 60 days—in the paper, on bulletin boards, in personal letters, and through line organization.

There was a good reason for this apparent split in thinking; namely, the manager's in-

---

* Even though a recent opinion survey had found that something like one third of his people thought his company's return on investment was 25 to 50 per cent. The actual figure was 11 per cent.

stinct that unrelieved, parrot-like repetition of the same words or ideas will in time lead to reader boredom and loss of attention. This is a sound instinct, of course. The more sophisticated the reader, the more likely he is to recognize quickly that he "has seen this before." It is not unusual for the editor of a well-conceived publication to receive a letter from an irate chemist asking, "Do you realize that, with variations, you have said precisely the same thing about profits six times in six issues?"

This should seldom surprise or alarm the editor. The point which a sophisticated intellect absorbed with one telling is only beginning to penetrate the outer edges of consciousness in most of the publication's audience. The average reader does not reach out for ideas; they must fight their way through to him, and few make it on the first try. This means that repetition is basic if employee publications are to be used with maximum effectiveness.

But repetition should never become mere hammering or sloganizing. Varying the form, style, and manner in which an idea is expressed is required to prevent reader exasperation. Over a period of time, for example, an employee publication may reiterate an important point by presenting it through a formal statement by management; through a picture and caption; a news story; an editorial; a cartoon, or any one of numerous editorial devices. In some guise, however, facts and ideas must be repeated if they are to register with large numbers of people.

2. WHAT DOES IT MEAN TO ME?

A second basic technique of persuasion is to tie the problem and the need for a solution to the employee's self-interest—to show that the subject being discussed concerns not only "other people," but the individual employee as well. No man, however altruistic, feels another's problems as keenly as he feels his own. It is always important to emphasize the individual's personal stake in adequate company earnings or improved technology or conservation of operating supplies.

Even businessmen must be lured to business articles by suggestions that they are pertinent to the reader's own concerns. At hand, for example, is a recent issue of *Nation's Business,* published by the U.S. Chamber of Commerce. Its contents page describes 17 articles. Eight of these capsule comments contain the word "you"—that is, "Here's your stake in . . ." or "These tips will help you plan." Three titles of articles contain the word "you": "What You Can Do about Stress"; "Put Power in Your Words"; "Here's a Contest You Can Win."

Well-planned articles for employees frequently do the same thing. Examples: "Your Stake in Cost Reduction," which tells why employees should co-operate in a campaign; "They Keep You Competitive," an article describing the work of methods engineers; "You and Your Job," a feature selling quality workmanship.

This is not to say that "you" should appear in every story title; nothing could be deadlier. But it is important to remember that, if any article's relevance to employee interests is not clear and explicit, the piece will probably make little impression. Accordingly, many managements today counsel their editors to subject all important policy stories to the imaginary employee questions, "What do I get out of this development? What do these facts mean to me?"

Unless such conscious efforts are made to attract the reader, a problem of crucial importance to the organization may be dismissed by the employee as an abstraction with no importance to him personally.

3. MAKE IT VIVID

When you study a story which has "gotten through" to employees, you generally find that it stands out for its "vividness." Sometimes this quality is intrinsic in the subject matter—in announcements of pay raises, for example, or new benefit plans, a new cafeteria, a fashion story featuring pictures of pretty girls. Some subjects just naturally appeal. But most business topics do not prove so fascinating in their pure state. For one thing, business language is characterized by hard words and technical abstractions. The connection to live people of polysyllables like "obsolescence" or "renegotiation" is far from obvious. To understand these usually requires special knowledge or hard mental effort.

This means that the publication's job is not done if it states a subject as abstractly as it comes out of a managerial staff meeting where everybody knows the problems and the code words. The jargon will have to be translated into down-to-earth examples and concrete stories of specific people and events.

Consider the traditional management problem of acquiring worker acceptance of needed improvements in processes and technology. This has been a major task since the days 175 years ago when mobs of English hand spinners burned Richard Arkwright's mills. Yet an employee publication often treats this subject in general terms without any attempt to cite case histories. It affirms what is obvious to management: "Automation is a good thing," or "Improvements in technology prove beneficial to all." Such statements may be accepted, resisted, or ignored altogether.

The prospects for reader acceptance are much improved when the problem is stated in vivid, human terms. One employee publication, under a heading, "Cradle-Size Consumers," featured a large photograph of 50 mothers holding infants born to plant employees during a year's time. The caption under this attention-grasping photo explained that the local youngsters were among 20 million new citizens added to the U.S. population in five years; that their future health and well-being would demand vast quantities of goods; and that, with the work force declining as a percentage of the nation's population, the only way to produce the needed goods was to multiply individual workers' output. This, in turn, necessitated the constant search for new methods, processes, and machines, as illustrated by certain local developments which the publication cited in detail.

By the same token, the editors of a Du Pont publication, *Better Living*, sought to make the basic point that the American standard of living has steadily improved. Deciding to focus upon family diet as one evidence, they laboriously constructed an enormous display of the food consumed by an employee and his family per year. This task required several days of bleak and uncomfortable work in a cold storage warehouse. So vivid was the resulting picture, however, that it and the feature were reprinted by *Life* magazine, and the photo has been additionally reprinted more than 1,000 times. It may be assumed that the editors' work to make vivid an abstract subject paid rich dividends.

Obviously, making a story interesting is largely an editorial function. But there is one important point which the top manager can profitably keep in mind: he cannot hope to persuade people with abstract statements. Stories are best told in terms of people.

4. WHO SAYS SO?

A final requirement for registering an idea is that it must be validated. One must prove that what one is saying is so. There are two prime ways to do this. The first is to present readers with indisputable, verifiable facts—the kind of tangible proof which management itself would demand before agreeing to a course of action or policy.

Second, and just as important, a publication must document its opinions with quotations from management. "Who says so" is almost as important to reader acceptance as the actual merits of what is said. Obviously, the opinion of experts, distinguished persons, or men of authority carries far more weight than the sentiments of Joe Doakes. It is easy to overlook this simple point. For example, I have watched one company publication for three years for concrete evidence that its management subscribes to what is being said in print; obviously, all members of management shun direct quotation and prefer anonymous editorial exhortation. This is dubious technique, for nothing is stronger than to quote the president or plant manager as saying that "quality must be improved" or "competition is keen." This makes a far deeper impression upon employees than if someone farther down the line makes an identical observation.

In all the foregoing discussion, it has been stressed that successful use of the techniques of persuasion requires careful thought and painstaking work. Even more than these things, however, any business effort at persuasion must be characterized by integrity and responsibility. Neither a publication nor any allied form of activity can serve as camouflage or act as whitewash. Lincoln said that one "can't fool all of the people all the time"; today, in an age of mass communications, one cannot fool *any* of the people for very long—and most certainly, one cannot hoodwink one's own employees who can quickly measure what a company says by what it actually does.

Both content and techniques of a management program of persuasion must, therefore, be sound and true. People are most likely to identify themselves with an organization when they are convinced that the statements of its leaders are the truth unsullied by shadows of chicanery or underhandedness.

Perhaps business management might adopt as its basic policy the persuasive technique which Thomas Jefferson said animated the Declaration of Independence: the object, he wrote, was simply "to place before mankind the common sense of the subject in terms so plain and firm as to command their assent."

6. What a Publication Can— and Cannot—Do

1. FOUR POSSIBLE MISCONCEPTIONS

About any new and promising management activity, there is likely to gather a number of hopes and ambitions which can never be realized in practice. Particularly is this true in the field of employee publications where many managements are still feeling their way.

Many misconceptions have accidentally sprung from work by the very people who have done most to establish employee periodicals as part of the modern business pattern. In the desire to put journalism to work for industry, publications salesmen have frequently promised far more in tangible results than any information medium could be expected to deliver. For this reason, many of the 5,000-odd managements who have started publications in the past decade may be disappointed with a venture which has failed to live up to expectations.

Accordingly, it is appropriate, first, to make a realistic examination of just what a publication *cannot* do for an organization.

1. An employee publication cannot magically solve deep-down organizational problems of discord and hostility. On many occasions, I have chatted with visitors beginning a tour of industrial companies prior to launching a periodical. Often the traveler has said that his firm was starting an employee magazine as a way to "solve serious industrial and public relations problems."

Unfortunately, a publication by itself can do no such thing. It is not a magic wand, a wave of which will automatically dispel organizational friction. It is only a channel of information, an adjunct of actual physical efforts by leadership to change the conditions which have created hostility. If, for example, a company or plant lacks a loyal and well-trained supervisory force, if working conditions are poor or unsafe, if people are treated inequitably or like interchangeable parts of machinery, if management does appear to have fought bitterly against every employee gain—if such things are so and there is no semblance of mutual trust and respect between management and employees, a mere publication cannot heal the breach.

Deeds must precede the printed word. No organizational periodical can make bricks without straw. It can only help blend an assortment of individuals into a loyal and productive team when the raw materials of esprit de corps are already present, though perhaps not well recognized.

2. A publication cannot change a man's mind overnight. Sudden, dramatic revolutions in employee sentiment are possible, but unlikely, if only because of the role which habit plays in human affairs. Seldom do new ideas burst like thunderclaps upon the race; men do not change the furniture of their minds all at once, but only a piece at a time, over a period of months or years. Nearly three centuries elapsed between Christ's death and the recognition of the Christian Church

30

by the Emperor Constantine. The "capitalist" donned the frock coat, striped pants and top hat in the cartoons of the nineteenth century; he is still wearing them in newspapers today.

People absorb new ideas slowly, not only because they may sometimes conflict with previous beliefs, but also because it is usually easier to go on thinking as one does rather than struggle to fit a new set of facts into what one already knows. Or it may be that a different point of view is too difficult or complex to grasp easily. For example, although there is a wealth of information available, most Americans would be hard pressed to give even the foggiest explanation of such economic subjects as inflation, or the role played by improved machines in creating high living standards. When and if large numbers of people come to understand such things, it will be because the subjects are discussed over and over again.

There is no way to blitzkrieg the job a good employee publication undertakes. A short-term campaign may get quick, tangible results in a Red Cross or Community Fund Drive. But to build a thorough understanding of the function and needs of business institutions, the industrial leader, like the educator and the churchman, must be prepared for a long-term program.

3. A publication cannot be expected to woo an individual from his role in life, or to separate him from natural loyalties to work associates and social or occupational groups to which he belongs. Certainly it is not realistic to hope that, by a publication or other means, a man can be kept "dangling"; he will associate himself with some group in the organization—it may be management or the union or "no union" or some craft alignment. But to belong to no group is intolerable.

A large plant with a fairly pacific labor history, for example, found a new union leadership suddenly threatening it with a work stoppage. Management was doubtful that employees would actually agree to a strike. "Take men like old Joe," it said. "He's been around here 25 years. He knows us; he wouldn't go along with a strike."

But when the stoppage was called, management found that old Joe was lined up with the pickets—and so were all his fellow mechanics. He could not divorce himself from his group. A man "sticks" not merely because of social or physical pressure from his group, but because of his own need to belong and to fit in somewhere.

All told, it is probable that management cannot transform a man's allegiances unless it is prepared to provide a new group with which he can identify himself. Before he can leave one group, he must be able to join another: a wage-roll man becomes a salaried employee, or a chief operator becomes a foreman. If there is no change in his group, there is no change in his primary allegiances. He cannot stand alone.

4. A management cannot expect to measure its publication's impact by the same yardsticks it would apply to a production process. Sometimes, of course, a manager will get concrete evidence that his publications dollars are paying off; a periodical can point to a successful waste-reduction campaign it conducted, or to the way it has stimulated the flow of employee suggestions. But instances where it can be said without qualification that "the publication alone did this" are rare. No one can point precisely to the force that converted a lackadaisical employee into an aggressive and spirited workman. Was the job done by a newspaper article, a lecture, by something his wife said, by a bulletin-board notice, by the remarks of his minister on Sunday morning—or by a combination of all?

No one knows. To justify an employee publication, a management can only imagine the dire results if it made no attempts at all to interpret itself. It can speculate about what would happen if it did not undertake to keep employees informed; or if it trusted to the grapevine or the union, or someone else to interpret management policies and motives; or if it permitted the political demagogue to decide without challenge what is good for business and the country.

Having reflected thus, management can only use its best judgment and the tools at hand to try and create the kind of employee relations situation it believes would be desirable.

2. WHAT A PUBLICATION CAN DO

If an employee publication cannot perform miracles, what *can* it do that is worth the money it costs? Essentially, it provides a way by which leadership of a large organization can enlarge the circle of its confidence, emulating as best it can the owner of a small business who acquaints people working in the same room with his plans, intentions, problems, and goals.

A good employer of five men would win employee support, first, through his good actions. But he would also continually clarify his thinking, explain his policies, and demonstrate his good will. The situation for the good employer of 5,000 men would be similar except that he would lack an easy way to convey his ideas to his people. Of necessity, he adopts the written word.

What attributes of an employee publication make it a valuable substitute for the man-to-man interchange which would be the ideal situation? Three unique capacities of a periodical stand out:

1. A publication by its very nature can provide detailed information on a range of subjects which the individual supervisor has neither the time nor the information to cover. The editor of a house organ can roam the plant or company. Appropriately and easily, he can report to employees the sources of raw materials and the product's use in customer mills; he can discuss the impact of inflation or taxes upon the employee's company; the sales outlook for the year; plant power consumption; the breadth and variety of the group known as stockholders. He can interpret the annual report and humanize the bald statistics it contains.

By the same token, the editor can take individuals far beyond their own jobs and areas, shedding light upon occupations and functions about which employees know little or nothing. He can describe the task of the methods engineer who is working to improve the company's competitive position; reveal the range of skills represented by the organization's people; interpret the importance of the much-discussed modernization or expansion project.

There is, in short, practically no company subject which a publication cannot interestingly treat, and with profit to management.

2. A publication can say what needs to be said to employees with completeness and accuracy—exactly as management thinks it should be said. A good publication can insure that every member of the organization gets the same story, the same facts, the same interpretation. It can thus forestall the inevitable distortions which occur when any set of facts is transmitted verbally through a number of persons.

3. An employee periodical travels into the home. The message or information addressed to employees is also conveyed to the wife who plays a substantial role in shaping her husband's views about his company and job.

The wife's key role is well known to labor unions. No strike can succeed for long without the support of the family homemaker who very quickly misses the security of the weekly paycheck. When income stops, the wife soon begins to exert pressure upon her husband to return to work unless she shares his sympathy for the union's objectives.

By the same token, a wife can dampen the enthusiasm of the most loyal employee if she is hostile to management, ill-informed, or if she constantly expresses doubt or suspicion of company action or motives.

For such important reasons as these, most well-conceived employee periodicals devote considerable thought to attracting and informing the wife as well as the employee breadwinner. It is significant to note that, despite the obvious economy of distributing periodicals at the plant gate, fully half of the nation's house organs are mailed to employee homes. One chemical plant found in a reader survey that, by doing so, it reached not only the wife, but an average of two other persons per copy of the employee newspaper.

3. IS THE PUBLICATION READ?

Such advantages as those cited above would be of little value if the employee magazine or newspaper were ignored by its readers. The crucial question thus becomes, "Does the publication get through? Do employees take the time to peruse it?"

There are only two ways to tell: one is to examine the comments expressed both by the individual employees and by the supervisory force which is in closest contact with the readers. By its nature, the data obtained from such sources may be piecemeal or contradic-

tory; individual testimonies must be weighed carefully against the possibility that the employee or the supervisor alike may tell management what it seems to want to believe. But most organizations will agree that a well-trained foreman has a pretty good "feel" about whether or not his people are reading the paper. Thus, many encourage a systematic effort by editors to sample foreman opinion on this important topic.

The second way to discover whether or not the employee periodical is being read is to run a readership survey. Because opinion studies of this type are a rather complex art, it is best, where possible, to put the job in the hands of a professional opinion research firm. Otherwise, the results which emerge from a survey of readers may look encouraging, but, in reality, be meaningless because the poll was improperly conducted.

In any case, objective, well-done readership surveys convey beyond any reasonable doubt that employee publications pass the most important test: they are read. This appears to be true whether the publication is a company-wide effort or a local, plant publication.

The case of one large magazine, *Better Living*, produced by the Du Pont Company, is illustrative. This publication, founded 12 years ago, is distributed to 280 plant, office, and laboratory locations across the country. Because of its large, diverse circulation, *Better Living*'s policy from inception has been to assume that it competes for employee time and attention with all magazines, newspapers, and other communications media.

Accordingly, in a recent readership survey, the publication was placed in the context of magazine reading in general. Into a list of 24 mass-circulation magazines, *Better Living* was inserted. Among other things, employees were asked to check those magazines they ranked highest in terms of interest, and those they read regularly.

Eighty-eight per cent of the respondents picked out *Better Living* as a "favorite." Its nearest rivals were *Life* with 56 per cent and *Reader's Digest* with 53 per cent.

This conclusion was cross-checked by other questioning which sought to find out how often employees looked at the magazine. Some 93 per cent of interviewees reported that they "always" or "usually" read it, while 86.8 per cent indicated that they read "a good part" of every issue.

The reason for such sentiments became evident when employee preferences in reading matter were examined. Out of a long list of subjects ranging from home repairs to hobbies, employees picked "the company I work for and its people" as a paramount interest.

That findings on company-wide publications are generally valid for other well-edited publications is demonstrated by reader-polls on local, plant newspapers. Recently, an opinion research firm checked reader sentiment about publications produced on three plants located, respectively, in metropolitan New Jersey, rural Virginia, and a site near a large Tennessee city. Polled employees covered a proportional sampling of mechanics, chemical operators, office workers, and supervisory or technical people of diverse ages, service, and training.

A total of 88.2 per cent of the sampling reported that they "always" read their plant papers; 10 per cent said "usually." More remarkable, perhaps, was the surprising unanimity of employee sentiment from plant to plant, however much their individual papers differed in content and quality. At one plant, 94 per cent of polled employees said they read "most" or "some" of their newspaper; at a second plant, the response was 95 per cent, and, at the third, the response was 93 per cent.

The preceding results are largely duplicated by a questionnaire survey conducted by a newspaper on an organic chemicals plant in New Jersey. Reporting anonymously, 91 per cent of the respondents said that they always looked at their newspaper. Less than one per cent said they found it "lacking in interest."

After all the qualifications which must accompany any survey results are taken into consideration, one conclusion still appears to be justified: The employee periodical is read, and it is, therefore, a potentially powerful communications tool.

This does not mean that the employee-reader cannot be bored or put off by superficial subject matter or inept editing. Far from it. A publication which studiously avoids controversial subjects or coverage of news uppermost in employees' minds is bound to inspire disappointment and, quite possibly, derision and distrust. Studies and experience do suggest, however, that, if a publication forthrightly and completely provides the employee with substantial and pertinent information, it will be read. An important management message has a first-rate chance of getting through.

The prime thing that an employee publication *can* do for management, then, is to make contact.

7. Who Needs a Publication?

Whether or not a specific company or plant needs an employee publication is something no outsider can arbitrarily determine. Each management, after pondering the principles discussed earlier, must decide the question for itself. This is so not only because each leadership is the expert on its own situation; it is true also because, unless management truly thinks through the subject of employee publications, anything which it might spend on them may well be wasted money. A periodical must have management's thought and interest as well as an adequate budget.

This point is important because many employee publications have been started up for the wrong reason. More than once, a publishing venture has been undertaken because so many other companies are doing so. But the fact that Company A pays for a publication is no reason why Company B should install one, any more than it should unreflectively spend money to duplicate other attractive activities.

No management need worry that it is missing a bet by not sponsoring a publication until it decides definitely why it should put out one in its setting, and until it knows exactly what it wants a periodical to do.

1. POPULATION AND PUBLICATION

The larger a company or plant, the more likely it is that a publication will prove useful. After countless conversations with managements over the years, it seems to me that top men begin to sense they are losing personal touch with their organizations when population approaches 1,000. Thereafter, the gap between top and bottom widens, and by the time enrollment reaches several thousand, there is no doubt of the need for auxiliary aids to man-to-man communication.

At the same time, it must be noted that hundreds of plants and firms with employment under 1,000 nourish employee publications and pronounce them profitable. I know one organization of 98 people where a periodical has flourished for years, through bad times and good, and where issue costs per employee are 10 to 15 times higher than those in larger plants. To my observation that, in such a case, a publication is useful but not essential, the manager strongly objected. True, he said, he actually sees most of his people in person nearly every day. But the newspaper pays its way because it introduces employees to a range of subjects which would never come up in conversation—things they should know; further, it can cover such subjects with an appropriateness and depth which he himself could approximate only by a carefully prepared speech.

This is an exceptional instance. In most cases, employee publications are born, first, because management finds that close physical contact with people is impossible in view of the organization's size; and second, because the publication is a logical way to try to compensate for this problem.

2. A SUMMARY OF PRINCIPLES

Because there are no hard-and-fast rules in this field, the best way to decide whether to publish a new or revamp an older publication is to review one's own situation in the light of the fundamental principles discussed earlier in detail. The basic points are three:

1. The growth of ever-larger organizations as a prime characteristic of our society has created a situation where discord and misunderstandings easily spring up between top leadership and those farther down in the group. As organizations grow and as job specialization becomes a standard feature of work, the employee's identification with his enterprise and its goals is not automatic as it was in the days of close physical association between owner and helper.

2. The need for employee understanding, loyalty, and support is at least as acute today as it was a century ago. An organization whose members are proud of their association, of their work, and of themselves, is obviously more effective than one rent by suspicions, misinformation, and antipathy. Ideally, all the members of an organization should be brought to feel the close personal identification with the enterprise that was common several generations ago.

3. The modern organization will have to overcome the communication barriers of its bulk and complexity in an "artificial" way by a program of information which interprets to the employee: (a) what kind of organization he is part of; (b) what kind of people are at the helm; (c) how the organization feels about him and his job; (d) what current problems are; and (e) what each must do to insure organizational success.

In devising such a program of information, a good employee publication will be found to be one of the principal tools.

If, after reviewing these points, management decides to produce an employee periodical, it then faces the task of codifying specific objectives it will seek to accomplish. Four primary objectives, together with illustrations, are described in detail in the next section of this volume.

Then, when its objectives are firmly in mind, management will have to install the personnel, procedures, and organizational practices required to produce the effective publication it sees in its mind's eye. A step-by-step recital of a pattern evolved from actual practice which has worked extremely well is found in Part Three.

Part Two

A Portfolio of Illustrations

———◆━◆———

Publications at Work

A Portfolio of Published Articles
Aimed at Well-Defined Objectives

One of the best ways to gauge the capacity and potential of the modern employee publication is to study examples of good work being done in the field. Accordingly, the following pages are devoted to a portfolio of published articles, features and picture stories chosen from a sampling of periodicals.

The briefest glance at this selection quickly establishes that a well-conceived employee publication can provide authoritative information on a tremendous range of subjects important to management. More, it can do this job in a fashion that is interesting, imaginative and likely to make an impression on employee-readers.

But study of the portfolio also reveals a fact that is even more significant to publication-sponsors: a good periodical must at all times be animated by clear and conscious purposes. Behind each of its features lies a well-defined objective.

Such objectives may be expressed in various ways, but always they will recognize that publications were born to help compensate for the communications barriers that rose as organizations of all kinds grew larger, more impersonal and more complex. In essence, a good publication's function is to build a harmonious and understanding relationship between the individual and the organization of which he is part.

This means that a thoughtful organization periodical will set out to achieve four specific objectives:

1. Building the individual's pride in, and identification with, his organization.
2. Increasing the individual's knowledge of the nature, problems and needs of his organization.
3. Improving the individual's understanding of his role and function within the organization.
4. Enlisting the individual's aid in improving the organization's efficiency.

These four objectives, together with publication features showing actual efforts to achieve them, are discussed in detail on following pages.

Objective Number 1: BUILDING THE INDIVIDUAL'S PRIDE IN, AND IDENTIFICATION WITH, HIS ORGANIZATION

A strong organization is composed of people who are proud of their association. In business, church, and military formation alike, the satisfied and productive individual will feel that he is part of an organization that is important, honorable, and deserving of his loyal support. He refers to "my company," or "my church," or "my battalion"; his group's prestige, feats, and triumphs rub off onto him and are a source of personal satisfaction and pleasure.

As pointed out earlier, the size of modern organizations poses a serious threat to this desirable attitude. But if the individual's feeling of personal identification is permitted to disappear, the organization pays a heavy price. The industrial employee is likely to become an irresponsible workman; the indifferent church member stays home on Sunday morning; the solitary soldier goldbricks.

This means that a serious publication's first and abiding concern is to stir the individual's awareness that he belongs to an organization whose standards are high, whose character is worthy, and whose achievements are notable. If the periodical fails in this fundamental task, anything else it might attempt is wasted effort, for the individual will display little interest in, or sympathy for, the problems and needs of an institution to which he feels no strong personal ties.

Accordingly, a business periodical will constantly describe to its readers the company's production, sales, or research feats, and the contributions made by its products or services. It will convey that management is human and deeply concerned with employee welfare; it will point out that the organization is a good place to work, providing good pay, good working conditions, job training, and opportunities for promotion. By all such means, it will show that the company is an institution with which the employee can proudly identify himself.

That this basic publication objective is valid for all kinds of organizations is suggested by the features (*opposite*). A sampling of employee publication articles directed to the same goal is shown on following pages.

CAMPUS WAS TO BE IN SPANISH ARCHITECTURE, SHOWN IN DRAWING BY DENMAN FINK, WHO LATER TAUGHT AT UM

TEMPO Vol. 10 No. 2

THE UM PLAN: *something out of nothing*

after thirty-three years a university blooms,
but once it was palmetto, pine and promises

By Michael Thompson

■ "Announcement Is Made that the fondest hopes of Miami's best people are about to be realized, and that a great open-air University to be known as the University of Miami will, in the very near future, be an actual fact. The University will be one of the largest and finest in this country, capable of amply providing for the needs of 5,000 students. It will cost approximately $15,000,000, of which sufficient endowments have already been secured to insure its successful accomplishment."

George Edgar Merrick — a lawyer by training, a poet by liking, a land developer by choosing—announced these "fondest hopes" in March 1925. His prospectus told of a bold, 100-million-dollar plan which would turn a palmetto patch into "one of the most beautiful parks in the world" with the Uni-

versity as its heart. Euphonically, as would be expected of a poet, he called it the Riviera Section. George's father, the Rev. Solomon G. Merrick, had come to the Miami area around 1898, when he founded the 160-acre Coral Gables Plantation. Rev. Merrick's "plantation" became the City of Coral Gables, comprising 16 square miles. So it was with this heritage that George Merrick told the world of his plan, and, as if he had to prove his sincerity, he pledged $5,000,000 to the cause.

The legal nod came on April 5, 1925, from Circuit Judge Henry Atkinson, who granted the UM charter. Bowman Foster Ashe, dean of men at the University of Pittsburgh, was hired as secretary by Merrick's group. Ashe conferred with architects, drew up the curricula, and hired some teachers. The UM Plan was looking good.

POSTER BOOMED UM PLAN TO MIAMIANS

University Magazine

Jump Boots Symbolize Paratroopers Esprit

FT. CAMPBELL, Ky—The rock-and-roller who sings "Don't step on my blue suede shoes" doesn't have a thing on the Army paratrooper.

Few things arouse his ire like having his highly polished jump boots tramped upon. It's not because he's a dandy and lazy to boot, but because he takes a fierce pride in them as a symbol of courage and stamina, and as a visible diploma that he is a graduate of the tough Airborne School.

During the swashbuckling days of WW II, many a pseudo-paratrooper returned from pass minus the shiny jump boots he dared to wear, unearned. Now regulations prescribe that only the genuine paratrooper may wear them with the uniform in off-duty status. His bona fide is proven by his parachutist wings worn over his left breast, the airborne insignia on his cap, and his airborne division shoulder patch.

duced on the feet of hard-marching paratroopers than it alleviated as a shock absorber during jumps. Toes jammed against the rigid toe were injured by the unyielding metal.

Today's boot is essentially the same as that which came into use on the eve of WW II. It has a beveled, non-trip heel and the rounded edges of the soles prevent cutting or fraying of parachute suspension lines should they tangle during deployment—a fault the sharp-edged grommets had.

This boot and the soldiers wearing it have since proven they can take a lot of punishment during more than a dozen combat jumps behind enemy lines in two wars.

The man and the boot go together, say paratroopers everywhere. They advertise prideful skill, toughness of body and spirit, and readiness around the clock.—ANS.

Military Newspaper

Without Fear or Favor

Lawyers are again indebted to Mrs. Catherine Drinker Bowen for a fine biography of a great lawyer and judge. She has now added the life of Sir Edward Coke to her previously well-received biographies of Mr. Justice Holmes and John Adams. Probably no single English judge and lawyer molded the thought and philosophy of Anglo-American jurisprudence to the extent that Coke did. His *Commentary upon Littleton* was daily fare for young lawyers until the latter part of the nineteenth century. What Coke thought on a subject is still of more than mere academic interest to us moderns.

The English-speaking peoples have for centuries clung to the concept that ours is a government of laws and not of men. We prefer to live under rules that are

Professional Journal

Membership Tops 3,100,000 In New United Church

The United Presbyterian Church in the U.S.A., which is being formed this week in Pittsburgh, has more than 3,-100,000 communicant members.

Statistics released last month reveal a membership in the United States and Alaska of 3,037,825. An additional 64,747, chiefly in the West Indies, raise the total to 3,102,572.

Of this figure, 2,791,547 were members of the Presbyterian Church U.S.A., and 311,025 belonged to the United Presbyterian Church of North America.

Congregations of both former denominations showed a considerable (64,000) net increase over the 1956 combined total. This gain was more than offset, however, by the transfer of some

Church Periodical

Above extracts from a sampling of nonbusiness publications show how organizations in all fields seek to build members' pride in being associated with a worth-while institution. The university magazine chronicles to its students the story of its growth. The Army newspaper selects "jump boots" to dramatize an elite combat force with a proud record of bravery and achievement. The professional journal focuses upon the noble tradition of a group which works for justice "without fear or favor," while the church periodical reports to members that they are part of a large and growing denomination.

NEW PICTURES JUST RELEASED SHOW
VAST SCALE of DU PONT'S ATOMIC ENERG[

HUGE HEAVY WATER UNIT AT DU PONT-BUILT-AND-OPERATED SAVANNAH RIVER PLANT GLEAMS THROUGH THE SOUTH CAROLINA N[

CONSTRUCTION OF THIS ATOMIC ENERGY INSTALLATION, BEGUN IN 1951, REQUIRED ALMOST 1.5 MILLION CUBIC YARDS OF CONCRE[

The need to show the individual that his organization is one with which he can proudly identify himself is as compelling in industry as elsewhere. The first step a business organization will take to reach this goal is to point to the production, sales, service, or research feats that the organization accomplishes. For example, publication stories will feature the institution's products, show that they are useful and valuable, that they have a reputation for high quality and play an important part in creating the high American standard of living. Likewise,

FFORT

UCES VITAL MATERIALS FOR U.S. DEFENSE.

ntly the Atomic Energy Commission re-
d from its picture files photographs of
units at its Savannah River Plant
e), one of the most vital elements in
defense. It is the largest building proj-
ndertaken by man, and was designed,
and is operated by Du Pont. It covers
ground than the city of Chicago, cost
illion, had a peak construction crew of
0. The vast plant in South Carolina
med 126,000 carloads of materials, dis-
d 39 million cubic yards of dirt (enough
n a wall 10 feet high and six feet wide
Georgia to Oregon), required almost
lion board feet of lumber, 118,000 tons
nforcing steel, two million blueprints.
e government turned to Du Pont for
easons: First, Du Pont performed a
r "miracle of construction" a few
before (*next page*). Secondly, as a
company, it had available a huge pool
uable talent in its commercial opera-
Du Pont undertook the job, raided its
anks of key personnel and placed its
sive facilities at the nation's service—
id this for a fee of only one dollar.

FLARE TOWER, which burns off waste gas, soars high above the 315 square miles of South Carolina that make up the Savannah River Plant. In this area are 280 permanent buildings, five nuclear reactors, two chemical separation areas and a heavy water plant. Some 7100 people are employed in operations.

a publication will remind readers that the enterprise's history and traditions are notable, that its facilities are modern and its outlook progressive. An unusually dramatic example of a pride-building story is shown above, in which the editor reports that the organization placed its know-how and personnel "at the nation's service" to undertake an enormous defense project. The publication's object here was the same as it would be in a less spectacular story: to cite evidence that the individual's organization is a meritorious one that fully deserves his loyalty and support.

43

FIVE YEARS OF PROGRESS

Plant and City Grew After Debut of 'Dacron'

Five years ago, in March, 1953, the first commercial production of "Dacron"* polyester fiber at the spanking new Kinston Plant caused quite a stir—and it's no wonder. The oozing of that first staple from a spinnerette, followed by production of the first continuous filament yarn four months later, fulfilled many dreams and made good a bet of some $80,000,-000 that "Dacron" would succeed.

That's about how much Du Pont had invested in the slow and careful development of "Dacron" and construction of the Kinston Plant, which began in April, 1951. Since those eventful days, our new

man-made fiber has become familiar across the nation. With constant research, quality improvement and processing advancements have come scores of new uses for "Dacron" in clothing, home furnishing and various industrial materials.

The Kinston Plant, where all of America's "Dacron" is produced, has grown into a business with jobs for about 2,000 residents of 11 counties in Eastern North Carolina and a monthly payroll of approximately $1,000,000. In November of last year, Plant Manager W. E. Gladding reported that the Plant spent $268,965 to buy goods and services from 171 Kinston suppliers in 1956 and $544,380

more for purchases from 356 other North Carolina firms. Employees of the Plant also are aware of steady improvements in working conditions and numerous increases in benefits received through the Company's various Industrial Relations Plans.

The City of Kinston has grown, too, during the past five years; and much of the progress at the Kinston Plant is reflected in the social and economic life of Kinstonians and residents of surrounding communities. Exactly how much the Plant has affected Kinston—and Kinston, the Plant—is impossible to say. One thing, however, is certain: Both have marched forward, hand in hand; and the fifth anniversary of our Plant's operations is an appropriate time to consider some of the changes that have taken place.

The U. S. census revealed a population of 18,336 for Kinston in 1950. The present estimate by the Kinston Chamber of Commerce is 26,300. Since 1951, the area of the City has more than doubled with four extensions of the City limits, including the recent addition of Club Pines. More than 1,300 new homes, 11 new churches and three new schools have been built. More than 125 business firms, mostly small businesses, have been established. More than 40 men and women in professions, such as doctors, lawyers, accountants and architects, have set up practices in Kinston.

The following pages illustrate some of the changes that mirror progress in Kinston and at our Plant since the momentous debut of "Dacron".

The profound economic and social impact of a business enterprise is easily and often overlooked, even by employees of long service. Accordingly, most publications repeatedly seek to build readers' understanding and pride that their organization is a valuable neighbor and an asset to the community. The story reprinted here is notable for its detailed documentation of this theme: in five years, a new plant created 2,000 jobs, poured a $1 million monthly payroll into the area and annually bought nearly $1 million in materials from state and regional suppliers. At the same time, the city prospered as 1,300 new homes, 11 new churches and three schools were built, and 125 new businesses were started up.

PROPERTIED MEN, all of whom work at the Houston plant, meet with Mayor Mercer Burgin of La Porte, Texas (left), to discuss street-paving projects near their homes.† Lowell Brown, pointing, was instrumental in getting paved streets for his neighborhood in La Porte.

INSURANCE policies owned by Lowell Brown cover life, health and house. Americans like Brown own some $70 billion in life insurance.

CAR is "necessity" to Brown, although for many years it was considered luxury. Nation's people now own almost 50 million cars.

MAN OF PROPERTY

Until comparatively recently, property holding was limited to a select few who were set apart economically, socially, politically. For centuries, the great mass of people owned little more than the clothes on their backs. Strong conviction and determination that property holding should be open to all are not 200 years old. The means to that end is even younger. In the United States, where purpose and ability have been harmoniously wedded, where mass production and mass distribution have become realities, property holding has spread further and faster than in any nation in history. Old boundaries and distinctions, based on one's property, disappear and become meaningless as tens of millions of wage-earners like Lowell Brown, above, a pipefitter at Du Pont's Houston Works, become men of property and assume the responsibilities and enjoy the added satisfactions of their new status in the community.

HOME which Brown* owns is brick, has five rooms and separate garage. He paid $9200 for it in 1952. Until then, Browns rented. In U. S. today, more than 25 million families own their houses.

PROPERTIED MAN of Colonial times was William Penn, shown here negotiating a treaty with the Indians. He was one of the greatest land owners in American history. He was given a land grant in the East containing 48,000 square miles of the most fertile land in U. S.

MODERN APPLIANCES are owned by most couples like the Browns. U. S. buys more than seven million ranges and refrigerators a year.

CHECKING ACCOUNTS, a reflection of wide property ownership, are used by 40 million Americans like Brown, who banks in La Porte.

Prime evidence of an organization's worth is the economic and social welfare of its people. Thus a good business publication will repeatedly demonstrate that the modern industrial employee is a prime beneficiary of the sweeping material progress brought by an industrial society. Repeated features will show that his well-being is mirrored in his home, dress, diet, hobbies, health, family possessions, and the educational opportunities his children enjoy. The story here points out that mass-produced U.S. abundance has melted old social boundaries and distinctions by making the industrial employee a "man of property" and providing him with new dignity, stature, and importance in the community.

Let's Get Better Acquainted With —

Employee Relations Department

(One in a Series)

'They Concentrate On You'

To the passing motorist on Camp Ground Road, Louisville Works looks like brick and mortar and millions of dollars worth of production equipment, and it is. But it is more; its most valuable asset has always been, and will always be, the people who work here. What Du Pont President Crawford H. Greenewalt has said of all Du Pont employees is equally true of our plant's work force: That our enterprise is, in a very real sense, the sum of every individual's contribution, and its progress a measure of the abilities and skills of each of its people.

From Du Pont's first days on the Brandywine, one of the cornerstones of Company philosophy has been concern for the well-being of its people and respect for them as individuals.

The function of the Employee Relations Department through its five Divisions is primarily that of "concentrating on you." In the main this is carried out by helping the individual foreman or supervisor to "concentrate" in turn on the employees he supervises. Put another way, the Employee Relations Department may be said to be a "service" organization dedicated to the service and well-being of plant employees, continuing that concern for the individual felt by the founder of the company over 150 years ago when the work force was so small that he could be in daily contact with each employee.

On this page a sampling of the ways this is accomplished will make you better acquainted with the Employee Relations Department.

CONSTANT ATTENTION to the needs and welfare of the individual is the major concern of the Employee Relations Department through its five Divisions. In regular meetings of top department supervision, as in photo above, ways of accomplishing this goal are discussed. From left, clockwise, M. A. Waggoner, Community Relations and Training; C. H. Edwardsen, Special Assignments; Jack Dick, M.D., Medical; H. A. Hansen, superintendent; A. M. Mc-Connell, Industrial Relations; W. C. Moran, Safety and Plant Protection; and V. E. Senior, Personnel.

INDUSTRIAL RELATIONS. This division deals mainly with the administration of Industrial Relations Plans and Practices adopted by the company and designed to promote employee security. Usually this takes the form of assistance to the foreman or supervisor, when requested, and not a direct contact with the employee. One exception to this is in the case of an employee retiring under provisions of the Pension and Retirement Plan. Above, F. B. Cornett, left, talks with Jim Moss, Shipping, who retires on pension December 31, and Jim's foreman, E. E. Brunner.

TRAINING & COMMUNITY RELATIONS. This division includes the duties of producing and mailing to the employee's home the works pewspaper, and conducting training needed to prepare every employee to do his present job well and to prepare for future jobs. In his capacity as training supervisor, J. S. Hornbuckle, above directs programs aimed at development of personnel. Here he reviews with a group of foremen some of the basic needs and wants of employees in their daily living. Others, from left, Urbane Goines, C. C. McNeely, E. P. Chinn and H. R. Haysley.

One of the most unflattering and dangerous stereotypes about business organizations is that they are "soul-less"—heartless or careless "where people are concerned." Citing evidence that the truth is otherwise becomes an important job for the employee publication, which sets out to show that good faith with employees and thoughtful, individual treatment are cornerstones of successful business operations. The feature above, for example, begins by telling employees that they are regarded as the organization's most valuable asset, and it then documents the scale of plant efforts to train and develop personnel, to guard the individual's health, recognize his service, and provide him with maximum personal opportunity.

Vacation, Insurance Plans Liberalized

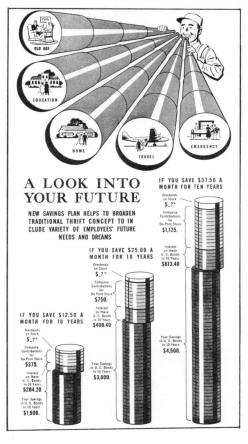

A LOOK INTO YOUR FUTURE

NEW SAVINGS PLAN HELPS TO BROADEN TRADITIONAL THRIFT CONCEPT TO INCLUDE VARIETY OF EMPLOYEES' FUTURE NEEDS AND DREAMS

IF YOU SAVE $12.50 A MONTH FOR 10 YEARS
Dividends on Stock $.?*
Company Contributions for Du Pont Stock $375.
Interest on these U. S. Bonds in 10 Years $204.20
Your Savings in U. S. Bonds in 10 Years $1,500.

IF YOU SAVE $25.00 A MONTH FOR 10 YEARS
Dividends on Stock $.?*
Company Contributions for Du Pont Stock $750.
Interest on these U. S. Bonds in 10 Years $408.40
Your Savings in U. S. Bonds in 10 Years $3,000.

IF YOU SAVE $37.50 A MONTH FOR TEN YEARS
Dividends on Stock $.?*
Company Contributions for Du Pont Stock $1,125.
Interest on these U. S. Bonds in 10 Years $613.40
Your Savings in U. S. Bonds in 10 Years $4,500.

3 Weeks After 10 Years' Service; Insurance to Equal Two Years' Pay

General Services employes are to receive three weeks' vacation after 10 years with the company and also have an opportunity to be insured for twice their annual pay under revisions to the company's benefit programs which become effective January 1, 1957.

Instead of the 15 years' service previously required, employes who have worked for Du Pont for 10 years are now eligible to receive three weeks' vacation annually. Du Pont men and women with 25 years' service now receive four weeks' vacation under revisions in the company's vacation plan made three years ago.

The company has had a Non-Contributory Group Life Insurance Plan in effect since 1919, and a contributory plan since 1952. Under the present plans basic life insurance of $3,000 was provided at no cost to employes. They also had the option of buying, at a low group rate, insur-

Jerry Perry, Power Engineer, Is 10,000th Co. Pensioner

We Must Keep These Scales In Balance

Some of the most dramatic evidence of management's concern for the individual's welfare is provided by the so-called "fringe benefits" that aim to help protect the employee and his family against present and future emergencies. Articles above on pension, savings, vacation, and insurance plans indicate the way publications will frequently remind employees of these benefits. An interesting variant is provided by the article, "We Must Keep These Scales in Balance," which reminds employees that benefit plans are not charity, but the fruits of steadily increasing productivity; future benefits, like past, must be paid for out of production gains.

21 Years Without Missing A Paycheck

There is good reason for Jim Aikens, Guard Force, to look mighty satisfied. Jim is standing behind a display of 562 of his paycheck stubs and pay envelopes—the total number of checks he received and stubs he saved as a Du Pont Company employee. This represents 21 years of uninterrupted pay starting from his first week of work as a Guard, December 31, 1936.

Jim has not missed a single paycheck or pay envelope since that time, including five absences (totalling nine weeks) due to illness. He continued to receive his pay dur-ing these periods through the Company's Disability Wage Plan.

More enjoyable, through the Vacation Plan, Jim has received paychecks during 48 weeks of relaxation—his total vacation time with the Company. In addition he has cele-brated 90 paid holidays.

Jim's 562 paychecks typify the experience of many General Services employees, reflecting good pay, steady work, and broad benefits which characterize a career with General Services and Du Pont.

SERVICE RECORDS OF EMPLOYEES AT LOUVIERS, COLO., EXPLOSIVES PLANT, WHICH MARKS 50TH ANNIVERSARY THIS YEAR, ARE IN CLOSE PROPORTION TO OVERALL COMPANY SERVICE FIGURES. LONGEST SERVICE—48 YEARS—IS HELD BY CHIEF CLERK GEORGE WIRTH (FAR LEFT).

FIFTY YEARS IN THE FAMILY
Colorado Plant's Golden Anniversary Marks an Era of Proud Association Between Du Pont and Those Who Made a Career With It

Desire for job security ranks first among employee concerns, and publications will accordingly stress both the organization's past record and its present efforts to provide stable employment. All job security stories should, naturally, be realistic, pointing out that in a free market economy, a company faces problems of market demand and consumer favor over which it has no control; it makes every effort, however, to avoid severe fluctuations and to adjust for seasonal variations in demand. Features shown here cite employee service records as evidence of security; top article reports a man who has not missed a pay check in 21 years, while lower piece shows that 45 per cent of one plant's work force has 10 or more years' service.

Good Working Conditions

A Photo Gallery of People Who Build Them in General Services

The barber was complaining: "Once you Du Ponters start talking about your operations, I can't get a word in edgewise."

It's hard to imagine THE BRIDGE's barber outmaneuvered in conversation, but, in any case, his words may reflect the time and attention General Services devotes to providing good working conditions.

For example, large numbers of our people spend many hours a year making our Department "a good place to work." Constantly improving working conditions and work environment is fundamental General Services and Du Pont philosophy. Because of the nature of much of our work—maintenance, service, construction, etc., obviously, physical surroundings may seldom rival the family living room, but the efforts of dozens of our people are aimed at making the work setting as safe, pleasant, and attractive as possible.

Pictured here is a sampling of General Services people engaged in such activity. Ranging from Painters to Methods and Planning men, they were photographed by George Maxwell in a recent tour around the Department.

"GOOD HOUSEKEEPING is a big part of good working conditions," Odell Hill said as he removed empty cartons from stock aisles at Stationery & Forms. "That was one of the first things my foreman told me when I came here. Not only is housekeeping important to better work, but, when things are in order, the place looks better. You feel better. All of us here at Eden Park work at housekeeping. We have the best looking warehouse I ever worked in."

PAINTERS—"A good paint job should both protect and please the eye," says Charlie Jackson. In the past six years, he reports, our painters have put at least one coat on "everything that's fastened down in General Services." Shown putting final touches to color-conditioning job in the Carpenter Shop, Charlie estimates that in a typical year our painters use about 4000 gallons of paint. Of all the jobs he's done, which was the most satisfying? "The overall color-conditioning we did in the basements."

METHODS & PLANNING ENGINEER Paul Allen made a study to replace obsolete pot washing equipment in the Hotel Kitchen which had an interesting sidelight. According to Paul, observing decibel meter with Bob Lightner, Power (center), "We found the noise level in the area not hazardous, but definitely uncomfortable to Connie Nacchia" (right). Paul added: "New equipment planned to be installed will be altered to reduce noise at no extra cost." No extra cost—just a little extra care.

REFRIGERATION MECHANIC Bob Bolen grinned when asked the importance of his job and working conditions. "You know," he said, "I don't know what people did in the summer years ago, before we had air conditioning. Take this job" (Bob had replaced a compressor in the air-conditioning unit in the Valet Shop) "When I got here to fix that unit, the temperature was in the 90s. The humidity made by the pressing machine was awful. You can really feel the difference, and there's the answer."

SERVICE OPERATOR Merritt Sipple, of the night cleaning crew, is responsible for keeping locker rooms clean and attractive. "I know how a man feels to have a shower after work and a clean place to keep his clothes and to dress," Merritt said. "After all, I use the place myself. How do I know it's important to good working conditions to keep locker rooms clean? You saw how little trash

SAFETY MEN—"Safety is a prime ingredient of good working conditions," says Hank Burchnall, shown checking Nemours freight elevator work with George Burris and John Vendrick, Engineering Section. "You might think that, after 10 Board of Directors' Awards in a row, Office Buildings Division is as safe as can be. But our goal is to eliminate all injuries, not just majors." Besides conducting inspections and tours for potential hazards, developing programs for safety meetings, Hank is con-

ELECTRICIAN Charlie Brooks is General Services' "hi-fi" expert. Charlie maintains all sound equipment in the Department, including the tape recorder, above, which sends music to work areas throughout the buildings. "A few years back an industrial study showed that people worked better and happier with music." Charlie said. "I

Demonstrating that the plant or company provides its people with the best possible working conditions is another way in which the employee periodical can help build the individual's pride in his organization. The above feature interestingly delineates management efforts to create a "safe, pleasant and attractive" work setting by photographing a cross section of individuals whose work is directed to that goal: painters, safety men, service personnel, electricians, and others.

PROMOTION REACHES EVERY LEVEL IN COMPANY

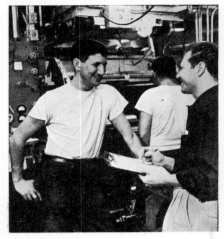

NEW OPERATOR Harold Adams, left, has duties explained by Foreman Leroy Martin. Adams started at Clinton in 1951, was packer, then helper before promotion.

NEW FIRST CLASS MECHANIC Roland Parker is greeted at home after advancement. He began as a helper at Clinton.

NEW AREA SUPERVISOR Eugene Petty watches Painter William Forsee put name on Clinton office. Petty joined Du Pont in 1934, supervises 204 men.

NEW KEYPUNCH TYPIST Teresa Pranger receives toast from Label Clerks Carol Martin and Rose Ann Potter, with whom she worked before moving up. She started her four-step progression at Clinton in 1953.

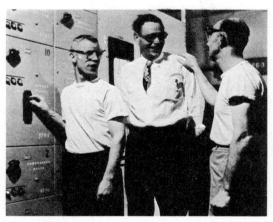

NEW FOREMAN Melvin Van Zuiden is congratulated by Operators Leonard Eversoll, left, and Edward Wedge in chemical building. Eversoll shifted to new Clinton job following Van Zuiden's promotion.

NEW SALES MANAGER Carl Schreep moves into desk at regional office of industrial film sales, Chicago. He formerly sold film in four-state area.

NEW SHIFT SUPERVISOR Harold Woomert, right, looks over jobs he now directs at Clinton. James Deutsch, assistant area supervisor, is at left.

NEW RESEARCH SUPERVISOR Robert Prengle packs books in Wilmington office before leaving for Buffalo laboratory. He joined Du Pont in 1953.

Objective Number 2: INCREASING THE INDIVIDUAL'S KNOWLEDGE OF THE NATURE, PROBLEMS, AND NEEDS OF HIS ORGANIZATION

If any organization is to function smoothly and harmoniously, it must take pains to insure that its members fully understand its goals, the way it operates, the problems it faces, and the conditions or climate it requires to perform its function. Providing readers with such information is the second major objective of a good organization publication.

Because businesses are economic institutions, they will be especially concerned to build the individual's knowledge of economic subjects that relate to industry's health and survival. Employees must be fully conscious that to stay in business, an enterprise must meet its competition, earn a profit, pay a return to investors, and keep its processes modern and up-to-date. More than this, employees should be fully aware of management's point of view on such broad questions as inflation, taxation, productivity, or automation. Only by providing its people with factual information on such basic topics can a company hope to dispel the myths, confusion, and wishful thinking that characterize most economic thinking. The employee publication is a highly effective tool by which to do this job, as examples on the following pages indicate.

Other types of organizations, naturally, will face other kinds of needs and problems. How they acquaint their members with such matters may be seen in the sampling of features on the next page.

Opportunity for advancement, like job security, is a top-ranking employee concern, and a well-planned publication will repeatedly show that the individual enjoys a chance to get ahead and realize his maximum potential. One of the editor's primary goals will usually be to demonstrate the organization's fundamental policy of "promotion from within." To do so, he will report not merely management advancements, but he will also focus upon the steady stream of upgradings and progressions in the lower ranks of the plant or company. The facing picture page is an effective promotion story showing a cross section of advances made by personnel ranging from plant operators and clerks to top men in sales and research.

The Advisory Council and

The Future of the School of Engineering

The Advisory Council of the Engineering School of Pratt Institute has been established to advise and assist the staff of the School in carrying out its program of revitalization.

At the meeting held Friday, May 16, 1958, on the campus, 24 members of the Council were present and became acquainted with the program of the School, its philosophy and its needs.

The Advisory Council now numbers 30, of whom 21 are alumni. The nine who are not alumni are interested in education in general, and Pratt Institute in particular. These men have been very generous in making themselves available at meetings, the first of which was held January 17, 1958.

The following is an abstract of the material presented to the Council at the May meeting.

The establishment of Pratt Institute was the material expression of its Founder's conviction that educated men and women were the prime ingredients of a strong and free nation. Mindful of existing educational opportunities, he stated that the Institute should supplement the efforts of the public and other private schools, rather than duplicate their work and compete with them. His was a trail-blazing venture in the educational field, and his statements to officials of the Institute and to faculty members contain repeated exhortations to do pioneer work. It is in this spirit that the present administration of the School of Engineering is formulating its plans for the future.

Since World War II, the startlingly rapid advan-

The engineering problems of the immediate future call for performance at a level totally beyond the reach of the graduate of the ordinary engineering curriculum. It is clear that the trend toward the splintering of engineering curriculum that was so strongly developed before World War II should be arrested. What is called for now is a reorientation of our curriculum based on a more natural division of engineering effort, which is functional in nature. The large state institution and the sizeable private institution cannot adapt themselves quickly to major curriculum changes. The Pratt Institute Engineering School is small enough and demonstrably flexible enough to make the requisite changes rapidly and successfully. We are already on our way toward the establishment of a powerful school of engineering dedicated to the education of the qualified few who will participate in the dramatic work of the future.

To produce graduates of the stature and caliber envisioned by the Engineering School staff, it is imperative that only the best possible high school graduates be encouraged to enroll at Pratt. The upgrading of entering students is already under way.

The Institute's acceptance of a properly qualified applicant does not insure his enrollment. Many superior applicants cannot attend college without financial assistance. Others, although they have no need for such assistance, will be influenced in their selection of a school by the scholarship aid which is offered them. If the Pratt Institute Engineering School is to hold its own in the strong competition for outstanding high school graduates, adequate scholarship funds are necessary. Such funds are

which must come from the operating budget of the school.

A school cannot be better than its teachers. Without a competent faculty, the finest of buildings and equipment degenerate into show pieces for visiting laymen. When the school's task is to prepare men for creative work on the frontier for engineering, then the qualifications demanded of a faculty are magnified immensely.

The teacher in such a program must have sufficient competence so that he is actually contributing to the development and extension of his field. Furthermore, he must possess a good understanding and appreciation of adjoining fields of knowledge so that he can, in his teaching, move freely across discipline boundaries to point out generalities and similarities which apply to what are generally construed by students as completely diverse situations. He must strive constantly to instill in his students the general fundamental viewpoint of engineering phenomena.

Aside from the obvious human traits which are, at best, difficult to assess, the teacher must have a demonstrated ability in his chosen field, best indicated by the Ph.D. Degree, publications and the desire to do research. Such men, while in short supply for both industry and education, will enter the teaching profession if the school can offer them not only a somewhat competitive salary but also, and more important, suitable working conditions and equipment, a superior student body and proper intellectual climate.

The equipment of any engineering school must compliment the talents and capacity of its faculty

University Magazine

Anti-Obscenity Action Pending Before House

People Urged To Write to Congressmen

Constituents are urged to communicate with their Congressmen in the interest of speeding action on anti-obscenity legislation pending in the House of Representatives.

Particular attention is called to a measure that would authorize the prosecution of pornography dealers at places where the obscene material is received. Under present law, persons who distribute pornographic material can be prosecuted only where it is actually placed in the mails.

South Jersey residents are asked to direct an appeal for action on pending legislation to Congressman Charles A. Wolverton, of the First New Jersey District, or Congressman Milton W. Glenn, of the Second District. Mr. Wolverton, whose home is in Merchantville, and Mr. Glenn, who resides in Margate City, may be

Church Newspaper

how ama functions

Within the headquarters building 600 employees carry on the daily activities of the Association—activities prescribed by the profession itself. Every one of the 43 councils, committees, bureaus and departments of the Association grew out of an expression

Professional Bulletin

Army Faces Dilemma In Congressional Criticism Of Its Tactical Vehicle Plans

If the Army goes ahead with plans to purchase $36,000,000 worth of M-151 jeep-type vehicles, as it presently seems determined to do, indications are that there will be difficulties with the House and Senate Appropriations Committees.

In reporting on the Defense Appropriations Bills, just passed, both Committees made it clear they are unhappy over the Army's plans for light tactical vehicles.

and STRAC forces. Also, that it aggressively pursue the rapid development of the platform-type vehicles in all categories."

The platform vehicles mentioned in the Committee reports start with the Mechanical Mule.

Contracts have been let with Willys Motors for 2,400 of these; 1,200 already have been delivered.

The First Marine Division took the

Military Journal

Sampling of nonindustrial publications shows how institutions other than business firms describe their structure, needs, and the problems they face. The university bulletin reports to alumni the need for attracting top-flight students and faculty to its engineering school. The church newspaper draws readers' attention to legislation related to religious ideals. The professional association describes its functions and services to members of the profession. The military journal points to a budgetary problem faced by the Army.

Our Plant Looks To The Future With Confidence

Plant Manufacturing Superintendent, Gordon R. White Answers Questions On Acetate Market Conditions

Last year each employee attended a meeting entitled "The Acetate Industry" at which business conditions were reviewed and a brief ex-planation was given of the economics of producing acetate in today's highly competitive condition.

"The Acetate News" here presents an interview with Manufacturing Superintendent Gordon R. White to help keep employees fully informed of the latest developments in acetate business conditions.

" . . . . we look to the future without fear."

Question: How did acetate production in 1956 compare with 1955?

Answer: The entire acetate industry pro-duced 192 million pounds of acetate last year, 38 million pounds less than in 1955, in fact, 1956 was the lowest production rate since 1946.

Question: How about current stock of yarn?

Answer: Because the acetate industry during 1956, we see a total of 55 million pounds pro-ducers stock rose 107 million pounds last year which is about 25% higher than in 1955.

Question: Does the industry as a whole suf-fer the same fluctuations as we have here at this Plant?

Answer: Looking at the yearly figures for 1956, we see a total of 55 million pounds pro-duced in the first quarter of last year, 39 mil-lion pounds for the second quarter, 41 million pounds for the third quarter, and 56 mil-lion pounds for the final quarter, so you can see our competitors are faced with the same

sonnel, but it is our only insurance of remain-ing in a competitive position.

Question: Regarding "Orlon", what is the proposed rate at Waynesboro Works?

Answer: The May Plant is currently produc-ing over 60 million pounds of "Orlon" acrylic staple and tow. It is anticipated that we will produce an additional 40 million pounds at Waynesboro Works.

" . . . . competition remains keen."

Expect Production To Continue At Comparatively Low Levels

The Niagara Plant will continue to operate with its belt tightened several notches, at least through the the third quarter. On the horizon: the glimmer of a possible fourth quarter up-swing. These opinions were stated by manufacturing superintendent Roy Mahlberg in an ELCHEM inter-view.

We will "continue for another quarter at the relatively low pro-duction levels experienced over the first half of the year," he said. However, one optimistic note: There remains a "possibility of improvement in some produc-tion levels during the closing months of '58."

"We hope that we will be able to stabilize at least at our present levels," Roy said.

revisions in our monthly require-ment for one plant product."

As of the moment, here's the run-down on how the plant's pro-duction situation looks:

The Sodium Shop, in full pro-duction since the beginning of June, should continue at capacity. This situation might seem para-doxical in that an expected rise in demand for sodium for use in the manufacture of tetraethyl lead has thus far failed to show itself. Also, the demand for sodium cyanide is down, as well.

"While anticipating future im-provements in the T.E.L. and cyanide pictures, we have been converting our sodium to sodium cyanide and using it to balance our ADN requirements," he said.

Roy reports no change in the sodium perborate picture since last March when ELCHEM last reviewed production prospects.

As a bright note in the Vinyl picture, the manufacturing super-intendent commented that efforts toward the development of a vinyl acetate monomer market are "starting to bring results" and that we hope for "steady im-provement" over the last half of this year.

An expected last-half upswing in ADN demand has thus far "failed to materialize" and the plant is operating considerably below capacity this month. "Very little improvement" is expected in the third quarter.

In concluding, the manufactur-ing superintendent pointed out that much of the plant's produc-tion is keyed to output by the nation's steel, automobile, paper, and textile industries and that a general business pick-up in these fields would tend to influence our production favorably.

" . . . . a switch to heavy deniers."

A basic step in interpreting a business organization to its people is to establish that the customer is boss, and that whether a company succeeds or fails depends upon the reception accorded its products in a competitive market. Two interest-ing examples of stories reporting market conditions are shown here; in both, the editor has interviewed a high-ranking manager, who describes the sudden shifts in market and customer demands, and points to the importance of quick adapta-tion to changed conditions. Steady work and broader opportunities for the employee depend on pleasing the customer—a fact the employee should never be allowed to overlook.

This Is General Services:

The Foreman's Job

Key Man on Industrial Team, He Is Vital Link in Line Organization

It has often been said that "as the foreman goes, so goes the plant." This recognizes the fact that the foreman is a key man on the industrial team. If he does his many-faceted job well, it is reflected throughout the organization. If he fails, the team is weakened in direct proportion.

In an attempt to depict some of the important responsibilities of a foreman's job in General Services, "The Bridge" selected one of our recently promoted foremen in the Engineering Section.

Nelson Husbands was called from his job as a Carpenter by L. F. Talley, recently retired Supervisor of Maintenance & Construction, and was told that he had been selected for the job of foreman in the Construction Area. With five years of service up his sleeve, Nels had eyed a foreman's job for some time — and he readily accepted the promotion.

Nels' first job here was Carpenter in Office Buildings Division. As he progressed from one assignment to another, he learned a lot about the importance of relationships with his foreman. Now, from another vantage point, he is finding out that the foreman's role is a demanding one, calling for a variety of talents.

He better understands the old saying that the foreman is the sergeant of the industrial army. As a member of first-level management, he is the principal link in line organization between employees and upper management. His job is not only to keep production rolling safely and smoothly; he also is the one directly responsible for giving to each employee the individual attention he deserves.

FOREMAN Nels Husbands captains a team of G. S. craftsmen and laborers as well as outside contractors engaged in construction throughout the Buildings. Part of the team, front row, l. to r. are Charles Davenport, John Wachter, Al Hofmann, Paul Kehrer, and Gail Lutton; back row, Jim Irvin, Hugo Viarengo, and Howard Whitten.

PRODUCTION of high quality at the lowest cost is a basic objective of foremen like Nels Husbands. Nels knows that continued success of our operations depends on satisfying the needs of our tenants. He makes a periodic check of work on Textile Fibers project with Paul Kehrer (center) and Gail Lutton.

TRAINING new employees like Carpenter John Wachter requires Nels' careful attention. A craftsman who learns the right work habits in the early days saves time and trouble for himself and his foreman. Nels shows John how to change blades in the power saw for a special cutting operation.

PAPER WORK takes a lot of Nels' time. He must keep an accurate account of construction time, employee's time. He must order, receive, check, and store material for his various projects, and estimate total cost of each job. To keep himself well informed, he must also read daily bulletins, memoranda, etc.

Although most business failures result from incompetent or inexperienced management, employees do not always appreciate the importance of qualified leadership in a modern enterprise. Thus, shedding light on the management function at every level must be part of any publication's efforts to provide employees with an accurate and rounded picture of their company. Frequently such features will be presented in the form of pictorial reports of the activities and/or responsibilities of individuals ranging from members of the board of directors to plant managers. In the interesting example shown here, the editor has delineated the job of the line foreman, who is responsible for the production, safety, training, and over-all functioning of his group.

Plant Buying

To Keep Our Plant Operating We Depend on Small Business

How big and little business depend upon each other is clearly demonstrated by the purchasing activity on this plant.

If, for example, you check the logbook at the Main Gate, you find that supplier trucks, most representing small business, enter the plant at the rate of 40 per day—or one truck every twelve minutes.

Then, if you talk to John Morrison, who keeps track of all the operational items stocked in Plant Stores, you find we buy some 13,000 different items, ranging from piano wire and welding parts to filter cloths and 7 kinds of cotter pins.

But the crowning evidence comes when you talk to Purchasing Supervisor Ralph Schmidt. He and his staff meet an estimated 2,600 supplier salesmen a year, most of them from small business. As a result of these contacts, they purchase for the plant some $36 million worth of supplies a year, or $138 thousand per day.

During 1955 local purchases from 705 vendors amounted to 23½ million dollars. These purchases included utilities, fuel oil, steel, lumber, cement, hardware, office supplies, chemical raw materials and the like.

Hour after hour, day after day, materials flow into the plant. The bulk is fantastic and could hardly be measured if piled in one spot. The fact that Purchasing issues more than 23,000 purchase orders a year gives some idea of our needs.

The case of the company as a whole further points up the intedependence of large and small businesses. Du Pont purchases from some 30,000 suppliers approach $3 million per day.

Though you may sometimes hear it said that there is a clash between the interest of small and large businesses, the facts indicate otherwise. Big business cannot exist without little business. One cannot exist without the other. We depend upon small business for reliable goods and services; they and their employees depend, in part, on large business for their livelihood.

A cross-section of the more than 700 local businesses who help to supply Louisville Works needs is shown below.

PLANT PURCHASING SECTION, headed by Ralph Schmidt seated, purchases materials for Louisville Works at the rate of $138 thousand per day, makes over 200 phone calls to suppliers and processes 90 purchase orders for every 24-hour period. Small businesses, many of them local, make up 80 to 90 percent of the firms from which we buy. Standing from left, Cal Kriete, John Roome, Betty Eades, Bobbie Hawkins, Janet Cecil, Wendell Embry, Pat Suell, Carlos Perkins, Alice Glenn, Herb Jarboe.

PURCHASING agent for Laib Supply Co. is A. J. Huber. His firm is one of six local businesses furnishing us valves and plumbing supplies.

GENERAL manager of Central Glass Company's Louisville plant is Mr. P. E. Botts. He supplies glass for desks, window replacement.

SAFETY equipment such as Scott Air Pak held by Clark Orr, manager, Orr Safety Equipment Co., is bought from his firm.

MACHINE shop owners Art, left and Ed Hartlage supply Louisville Works with fabricated parts, do work on motor armatures.

A worth-while employee publication will steadily work to clear away the many dangerous myths and the folklore that frequently cluster around business subjects. One of the most prevalent notions, for example, is that the interests of large and small businesses are antagonistic, and that small firms are snuffed out because they cannot compete with "giant corporations." Actually, the two seldom compete directly and their activities supplement one another. To make this point by showing that large manufacturing firms stimulate rather than eradicate small, the editor of the above article simply reported the activity of his plant's purchasing section, which bought some $23 million worth of materials from local, smaller firms and suppliers. Similarly, other editors frequently do stories that report how small firms, processors, and converters were created or expanded by a large company's product or plant.

Size Depends Upon The Job to be Done

George Burris, Engineering Section, has three youngsters: George, Jr., age 12, who is five-feet-three-inches tall; Billy, age 6, four-feet-two, and Barbie, age 2, two-feet-eleven.

Ask George which child is "the right size" and he'd laugh at you. A ridiculous question. "Right size for what?" he'd want to know. For learning how to quarterback the Split-T, young George is obviously the right size. For balancing a two-wheeler bike, watch Billy who will soon be saying, "Look, Daddy, no hands!" For taking slow cautious steps down that steep stairway? That's the job of Barbie who will soon master this difficult feat.

"They're all the right size," George will tell you. "What's important is that they're healthy, and growing, and learning all the time."

This common sense philosophy, shared by parents like George, is one that might well be applied to the heated discussions of business size you frequently hear. What is the right size for a business? The only way to decide is to repeat George's question: "The right size for what?"

Business size is determined by the products a company makes and sells, and the processes necessary to both. The assembly of automobiles, the metallurgical reduction of steel from its ores, the manufacture of a wide range of chemicals can be efficiently carried on only by large businesses. On the other hand many services, sales and some types of manufacturing can best be done by small businesses.

Are they healthy? Do they do the job well? Are they learning and improving as they go? These are the questions to be asked of American business, large and small.

Which Child Is The Right Size?

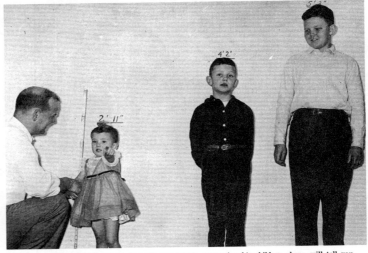

SIZE MEANS NOTHING by itself, as George Burris, measuring his children above, will tell you. Barbie, left, can't ride a bike; Billy would be inept at quarterbacking; and George, Jr., is a long way from a pro. But each is doing the "right" thing for his size. You must judge size by function.

All Kids Are The Right Size...

RIGHT SIZE to advance from toddling up the stairs to pioneering in the awesome downward descent. In a few brief weeks, Barbie will have mastered "going down" and will be ready to tackle another learning problem.

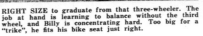

RIGHT SIZE to graduate from that three-wheeler. The job at hand is learning to balance without the third wheel, and Billy is concentrating hard. Too big for a "trike", he fits his bike seat just right.

RIGHT SIZE for learning the "Split-T", George, Jr., will be ready in a couple of years when he starts high school for more earnest training. As he barks the signals to his buddies, he learns the value of teamwork.

Of all the "big" institutions that characterize our society, the business organization is the one most likely to be assailed for its size. Its growth is often considered as an isolated fact, without reference to the corresponding growth of population and to the needs which called it into being. Because it is proposed from time to time that businesses be made to conform to some arbitrary, "desirable" size, the thoughtful employee publication will frequently remind its readers that a business's size is determined by its function—by the demands of the products it makes and the scope of its processes. The story printed here makes this point interestingly by showing that there is no arbitrary "right size" for a child just as there is none for a business. Whether a firm is small, medium, or large depends upon what is required for the job it does or the service it provides.

PROFITS PROVIDE JOBS—Ed Quinn, "Freon" operator and Bridgeton resident, has been collecting DuPont pay checks, as in this scene, for 23 years. He is one of over 6500 Chambers Works employees whose jobs were created through stock investment by people who seek a reasonable return on their money. Without the opportunity for a fair profit, there would be no investment, and no job.

The "Profit Squeeze" ... and You

There is a great deal of talk in the newspapers these days about the "squeeze on profits."

Essentially, what this expression means is that business costs — for wages, materials, tools, etc.—keep going higher and higher. Selling prices—the return business gets for its products—are going up too, but not enough to cover the rise in production costs.

The result is that profits are caught in the middle—they are "squeezed."

A close-up example of this general industrial problem can be seen in statistics on employee compensation. In DuPont, between the high level year of 1950 and 1956, wage and salary payments rose 62 per cent even though the number of employees rose only 12 per cent. During the same period, the company's net income rose less than 25 per cent although the average operating investment was up 60 per cent.

This is only one example. Other sharply rising costs include raw materials and tools. But wherever they come from, climbing costs must be compensated for by climbing productivity— improved technology and greater production. The only alternative, higher selling prices of products, is a poor substitute, for it tends to shrink rather than widen markets.

PROFITS SUSTAIN SECURITY—The brand of job security and steady pay checks represented by this photo stems from DuPont's ability to earn a profit over the years. Here, Julian Lucas, Azo Area operator, right, receives his 20 year service pin from supervisor Earl Duke. Lucas, who started at Carney's Point Works and transferred here in 1945, has shared in the plant's prosperity. He owns his home at Highland Ave., Pennsville.

An adequate profit is the fundamental and absolute requirement for a successful enterprise; a useful publication will continually stress this oft-distorted fact of business life, pointing out that management, employees, and stockholders alike have a personal stake in whether or not there are sufficient earnings. In the above feature, the editor has described the problem of the "profit squeeze," in which he reports that sharply rising costs of labor, raw materials, and tools without corresponding hikes in output and sales have squeezed profits to dangerous levels. To show that this threat is a danger to all, the editor points to profits as the force that creates jobs, sustains security, and provides tools and opportunities for advancement.

'Automation'

Age-Old Trend Means More Goods, Less Toil

Eli Whitney's cotton gin, invented in nearby Georgia, saved South's economy, boosted textile industry.

"Automation" is a word so new it hasn't found its way into many dictionaries. Automation itself has been around since the Stone Age man discovered he could roll a stone more easily if he applied a stick as a lever. To some, it means the manufacture of a product "untouched by human hands"; others tie it to electronic devices that "think" what to do and when.

But whether automation means a push-button factory or a simple conveyor belt, its object is to en-

"... a popular protest ... of the horses."

able men to produce more things, with less toil.

Many of the things automation—or instrumentation or the mechanical age—is producing are the luxuries that are unknown in places where technical skills have not been developed. The refrigerator—a neat bit of automation itself—would be available only to a wealthy few were it not for mass production techniques that are a part of automation.

Assembly lines brought autos to the masses in America.

In spite of its deeds, automation has not always been popular. There was a time when mechanical looms were considered to be undermining the livelihoods of the people. (When 18th century workers jammed their wooden shoes—or sabots—into looms to express their distrust in mechanical devices, the word "sabotage" was invented.) Horses made no audible protest when steam engines began producing energy measured in horsepower, but some saw steam as a rising threat to humanity.

The prophets who predicted that mechanization would leave the working man without jobs would find little support for their fears in today's mechanical age. The fact is that wherever instrumentation and automatic controls have been introduced, employment has increased. Nowhere has automation been applied so successfully as in the chemical industry, yet employment in the chemical industry has increased more than in the industries where old methods prevail.

Dial telephones have not reduced the number of human operators—there are fewer operators per telephone, but there are millions more telephones. Automation has made more things available to more people at lower costs, creating additional jobs. Not only are more jobs created, but better jobs. Greater skill and higher production bring with it a higher pay check. The man who once worked behind a plow must now operate and maintain a tractor, tilling many times as much acreage. The individual who once

made pretzels by hand has now mastered the machine which produces 50 times as many pretzels. He may be the mechanic who keeps it working. Or he may even be manufacturing—or designing—pretzel manufacturing machines.

Today's generation, which knows automation to be desirable, may live to see the day when automa-

Automation helps Lodema Stone, Technical, in many ways.

tion will be indispensable. U. S. population by 1976 will reach 216 million. But the work force will be only 30 per cent larger. The nation, at today's rate of output, would be able to produce only 70 per cent of the goods and services demanded. There would be a shortage of 76 million man-hours of labor in 1976.

The answer would seem to be to increase individual output. Automation does just that.

Automation Can Perform Jobs Humans Can't

In few places has automation come into its own as it has at Savannah River. There's no exaggeration in saying that the Plant and the jobs it provides would be impossible without automation.

Automation is particularly useful in performing certain tasks in some areas where robot-like machines do the work of many men. Because of the precise control required in the processes of the Plant's heavy water facilities, automatically-controlled instruments also play a major part in that phase of operation, as shown in these photos.

A handful of men can operate millions of dollars worth of equipment. Production men, Burne Combes, Cecil Scruggs and G. E. Thompson keep constant watch, interpret data and spot trouble. Automation permits them to work in comfortable surroundings, using their brains rather than their backs.

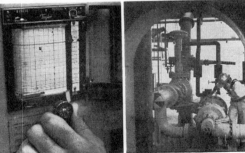

Simple devices ...   ... control pumps

Instruments Foreman Ray Cook is one of group which keeps many instruments working properly. Though instrumentation does the work, it requires skilled attention and has brought into being a whole new occupation.

One of management's perennial concerns is winning employee acceptance and support of technological advances—of the constant innovations and improvements in processes and equipment. Fear that "the machine" might throw people out of work is at least as old as the Industrial Revolution, and the problem has been intensified in recent years by scare publicity focused on the word "automation" and by a spate of stories about "workerless factories" and future mass unemployment. Accordingly, a good employee publication will repeatedly address this basic industrial subject. Stories on the pages above show two effective treatments. A feature entitled "Automation" (*left*) attempts to put technology into perspective, showing that the search for better and more productive tools has

ECONOMIC DILEMMA OF 1976 IS POSED BY TRACING DEMANDS VS. ANTICIPATED WORK FORCE.

Labor Shortage Ahead?

When the sons and daughters of Du Pont employees at Martinsville, Va., in the photo left, enter the work force at age 21 in 1976, the U. S. will be 200 years old, and could face one of its greatest problems.

For the simple arithmetic is that if the trends of the past 80 years continue, then the anticipated 216 million U. S. population of 1976 will demand twice the quantity of goods and services available today. Yet the work force 20 years hence will be only about 30 per cent larger than it is today.

What this means is that, at today's rate of output, the nation would be able to produce only about 70 per cent of the goods and services de-manded. Translated into time, there would be a shortage of 76 billion man-hours of labor in 1976.

This leaves three choices: Work 11.5 hours a day, or 57 hours a week. Attempt to recruit more labor among students, retired persons and house-wives. Or increase individual output.

Since the first two courses are clearly unlikely by present American trends, the real answer lies in the third—in utilizing every technical advance, every ingenious invention, every new tool to in-crease productivity so the available labor force can fill the 1976 demand for $750 billion of goods and services. The basis for achievement exists; the question is how the nation nurtures its prospects.

ANSWER TO SHORTAGES must be more output per hour. Using as symbols the nylon he helps produce, James Chapman, polymer and spinning operator at Martinsville plant, traces improvement in productivity (i.e., output per man-hour) for all U. S. manufacturing since 1936,* and indicates nation's output must virtually double through technological gains, if 1976 demands are to be filled.

meant more goods and less toil, and that throughout history, the material well-being of civilization has been proportional to the development and utilization of technology. Feature on the right shows that technology must be improved to take care of the needs of our rapidly expanding population; in 1976, the editor says, the U.S. population will demand twice the goods we produce today, yet the work force will be only 30 per cent larger than it is today. The result is that the nation must utilize "every technical advance, every ingenious inven-tion, every new tool to increase productivity" so that the 1976 demand for goods and services can be met.

STAGE SETTING FOR

The individual taxpayer, contemplating the impact of taxation on his income, might well pause to view the problem as it affects the modern corporation, and ponder the implications it has for him. Here, arrayed upon a stage in Wilmington, Delaware, are the 60 people and the battery of machines and records required to meet the tax obligations of a single U.S. corporation, the Du Pont Company. The tax bill for Du Pont for 1956 totaled $285 million. With almost 90,000 employees and a sales volume in 1956 of $1.9 billion, Du Pont is large, and it is understandable that its tax affairs are intricate. But the significance of these people is found not so much in corporate size as in corporate function. In essence, the company they serve is not only a taxpayer but also a tax collector. Just as they make individual tax deductions from the wages

With taxes absorbing some 25 per cent of the U.S. Gross National Product, a good employee publication will provide its readers with a steady stream of factual information on the size of the tax load, its impact, and the problems it poses for individuals and corporations. Such stories will usually seek to register such basic points as the following: (1) taxes are necessary to maintain society, but if levied unreasonably can easily become destructive by killing the creative individual's desire to excel, and the business organization's incentive to invest in new products and plants; (2) taxes are paid by people; there is no scapegoat to whose shoulders the burden can be shifted. Taxes levied on companies are as

RPORATION TAX BILL

Du Pont pays its employees, the people pictured here deduct for corporate taxes some portion of each dollar paid Du Pont by its customers. Taxes, like wages or raw materials, are a cost of doing business, and high corporate taxes are reflected in the prices consumers pay for products. In prosperous 1939, for example, Du Pont's tax bill was $22.1 million; net return on investment was 9.8 per cent. The years 1952 through 1956 also were prosperous, and the average return was less than one percentage point higher. But Du Pont's taxes were 13 times as high. Other companies have had comparable experience. What happened is plain. Industrial efficiency increased. But only part of the gain could be passed on to consumers in the form of lower prices —taxes took the rest. The burden thus fell on consumers as well as corporations.

much a cost of doing business as meeting payrolls and buying supplies. Since a company's only income stems from sale of goods and services, higher costs resulting from taxes are ultimately reflected in prices, and that means the consumer pays the bill; (3) in the long run, the only way to reduce taxes is reduce government expenditures—either that or hold expenditures steady and increase the nation's output so that taxes take a smaller share of the total national product. In the picture reprinted here, the editor has dramatized the magnitude of the tax problem by showing the number of people and machines required merely to handle one company's tax bill.

VALUE OF A DOLLAR

Inflation Obscures 40 Per Cent Rise in Du Pont Real Wage Since 1948, Matching Any 10-Year Gain

In U.S. supermarkets, Du Pont families currently find a telling lesson in basic economics. Their dollars buy less — the 1948 dollar, for example, is worth but 90 cents. But a day's pay buys more food — 49 per cent more than in 1948.

This paradox, seen here in the varied shopping experiences of the James Bolens of Flint, Mich., derives from these facts: Since January 1948, prices have risen on most consumer goods

(average increase: 18 per cent). But wages and incomes also have risen since 1948—and in almost every case at a faster clip than prices. The Du Pont average is up about 65 per cent.

The result is that the typical Du Pont employee has more than kept abreast of the increased cost of living. Now he can buy nearly half as much again for his day's work as in 1948, matching the gains of any decade in history.

When a dollar buys less, "inflation" is at work. That is what has been happening to the U.S. dollar since World War II, and there is a distressing threat of further inflation. But as the monthly changes of the "consumer price index" become front page news and a lively thermometer of inflation, they frequently obscure the fact that the real value of industrial wages—what they will buy—has climbed steadily. The James Bolens and families like them the country over have seen their purchasing power rise because new and better tools have provided them the means to make more and thus earn more.

LESS FOOD FOR DOLLARS SPENT SHOWS HOW DECADE OF INFLATION HAS ERODED VALUE OF DOLLAR, POSING CONTINUING PROBLEM.

WHAT'S THE ANSWER?
"Cost Of Living"

Question: Are food prices responsible for the recent rise in the cost of living?

Answer: No. Commerce Department studies show that food prices have increased only slightly over a year ago.

Question: What is the price picture on clothes, then?

Answer: Clothing prices have risen very little. Other items in the category of what economists call "non-durable goods"—oil, gasoline, home fuels, cigarettes, household textiles, etc.—are also at year-ago levels, or up very little.

Question: Can we blame rising costs on such things as cars, household appliances, and furniture?

Answer: No. The costs of most of these items, called "durable goods", have gradually dropped in the past few years. Prices actually paid for new automobiles have increased some, but these increases have been more than offset by decreases in costs of appliances and furniture, and by improvements in the quality of the cars offered.

Question: If none of these things is responsible for higher living costs, then what is?

Answer: Living costs have inched up because of steep and steady increases in the cost of what experts call "services and shelter." This category includes a large variety of expenses: Prices of houses, rent and home maintenance; taxes; medical care; education, insurance, interest charges; haircuts, and cleaning bills; auto repairs; and utilities, such as gas or electricity.

Dollar Value Cut By Wage Inflation

Question: Newspapers speak of "wage inflation." What is it?

Answer: When wages rise faster than output per man-hour, and prices are increased to compensate for higher wage costs, the value of the dollar is lowered; that is, a dollar buys less. This is called "wage inflation."

* * *

Such serious economic problems as inflation, with its impact upon industrial and personal budgets, are subjects that a useful organization publication will constantly strive to illumine for readers. Basically, most inflation features will register the point that the measure of a wage is what it will buy. Three approaches are reprinted above. The first (*top*) shows that although inflation has cut the dollar's value, employees' real wages have actually climbed. Article (*bottom left*) emphasizes that the rising cost of living is due largely to climbing costs in the service industries, where productivity increases much more slowly than in manufacturing. The third feature describes "wage inflation," caused by wage increases in excess of productivity gains.

SUBTRACTION ADDS UP

... To a Better Belle Works As Ammonia Modernization Calls Into Account Depreciation and Obsolescence

Coal Partial Combustion   **Thylox**

Coke Plant

Ammonia production, the key to Belle Works for more than a quarter century, is being modernized today so that in a few short years facilities here will rank with the best in the country.

Bringing ammonia up to date involves (in many of modernization's aspects) more a matter of taking away than of adding. The facts of contemporary chemical manufacturing life are clear on this: compactness, efficiency, modern methods — all relate to greater yield per dollar invested for the company and to greater yield per hour invested by the man who is doing the operating. Accordingly, there's going to be more room in the ammonia area. By the time modernization is complete, both Number One and Number Two gas holders will have ceased to function in their present roles. Number One holder is gone now. Number Two, now used for storage of "blue gas," will be switched over to handle nitrogen.

The Gas House and Coke Plant will ultimately be removed. The complete conversion of ammonia to natural gas will outmode their functions. The present Natural Gas Partial Combustion Unit and the water gas operation are now being replaced by an entirely new system which will produce our process gases with increased efficiency. Thylox? It's not longer needed because of the cleanliness of natural gas. The same is true of the caustic plant. Modern techniques call for its removal and Liquefaction will go with it.

Turn the page for a look into the future of Belle's ammonia producing facilities.

Gas House

DEPRECIATION and OBSOLESCENCE

Q: What's the difference between "depreciation" and "obsolescence" on a plant like Belle Works?

A: "Depreciation" at Belle Works means the same thing as it does in the home. When we say equipment "depreciates," we mean that its value declines as it gets older and wears out. For example, an auto you buy is worth less and less each year you own it until eventually it is scrapped. The same thing is true of a lathe or production machinery on the plant.

Q: "Obsolescence" is something else entirely, then?

A: Well, old age is not necessarily a factor in obsolescence. A piece of equipment is obsolete when it has been outmoded by, or is less efficient than, a newer method or machine. The obsolete equipment may be in perfect working order — but it has to be replaced, rebuilt or remodeled to meet competition.

Q: You mean brand-new items can be obsolete?

A: Yes, especially in the chemical industry where competition is intense, and where companies are constantly trying to produce better and cheaper products. It's even possible for a whole process to become obsolete if someone figures out a better, more efficient way to make the product you're making.

Q: What financial provision does the company make for worn-out or obsolete equipment?

A: Each year a portion of the original cost of plants and equipment, representing annual depreciation and obsolescence, becomes a part of the cost of the products sold, the same as labor and raw materials. These costs must then be recovered through sales of the products. Last year, the cost of depreciation and obsolescence came to 6 cents per sales dollar, or a total of $115 million.

Q: Setting aside proper amounts of money for replacement is quite a problem in itself, isn't it?

A: Yes, largely because inflation has raised replacement costs. For example: Imagine that a $200,000 piece of equipment installed in 1937 had an expected useful life of 20 years. So $10,000 a year was added to the cost of the company's products sold so that by 1957, when the machine wore out, its original cost had been recovered. Here's the catch: The same machine may now cost $400,000 or even more.

One problem that faces all companies is keeping facilities modern and replacing worn-out or obsolete equipment. Employee publications will therefore work to acquaint employees with the scope and expense of this pressing competitive requirement, pointing out that jobs and promotion opportunities hinge on keeping a plant modern and efficient. Article reprinted here describes modernization plans that will improve a plant's competitive position and shows how the organization provides the money to do the job. The editor also points out that inflation has magnified the problems of depreciation and obsolescence because an item of equipment today may cost twice as many dollars as was foreseen.

Plant Has Cut Its River Pollution By 70 Per Cent In Past Five Years Recent Report Reveals

Five Years Of Progress Is Announced

Industry Is Doing Its Best To Curb Its River Wastes

Waynesboro Works has cut its river pollution by 70 per cent in the past five years through diligent study, revamping its equipment, and a "fine cooperation on the part of our operators", according to Dr. Roy McCracken, Works Technical Specialist, who was recently a featured speaker at the Manufacturing Chemists' Association meeting in New York.

His speech, released today, outlined the results of five years' work in cutting our plant's B.O.D. (biochemical oxygen demand) poundage from 12,000 pounds to 3,200 pounds daily.

His speech, which was given at the Hotel New Yorker before the Air and Water Pollution Abatement Conference, showed how our plant has dropped its average daily pollution load to around 3,200

THE MAN AT THE METER determines how successful our pollution curtailment program can be. Garnet Thompson of Acetation is shown checking the acid meter near his station. He is always careful to keep the tanks from overflowing, and is our first defense against acid spills.

The growth of communities and their proximity to industrial plants frequently create problems and concerns in air and water pollution. Companies therefore want to keep the community aware that industry is attempting to do its part in solving what is a joint problem. In the story above, a plant newspaper presents a remarkable progress report that clearly conveys the organization's desire to be a good neighbor.

Why Import Unemployment?

Misguided U.S. Tariff Policy Threatens Jobs

Last week—and last week was not unusual in this respect—about 350,000 pounds of dyes were imported into the United States. There were imports of gamma acid from Japan, azobenzene from England, isocyanates from Germany and Holland, petroleum additives from Japan, MNPT and rubber chemicals from England, and, of course, the regular importations of indigo grains from Germany. This latter shipment totaled about 200 drums.

The dye industry is essentially a batch operation requiring a lot of manpower. This industry, particularly in Germany, Switzerland, England, France, and Italy, is highly developed and methods of production are practically the same as in the United States. The big difference lies in wage rates. A top chemical operator in a German plant receives 70 cents an hour. But the same man in the U. S. doing identical work receives from four to five times

competing with those of Chambers Works to enter this country from across the waters.

Few subjects are more controversial or less understood than tariffs. Few subjects have been more beclouded with foggy thinking. Succeeding issues of the "Chambers Works News" will attempt to strip away the haze, and show:

. . . That every pound of competitive product brought in from abroad reduces by a corresponding amount the American chemical

Winning understanding of the many kinds of special problems that affect particular companies or industries is another function of the employee periodical. Such problems are perhaps typified by tariffs. Article (*above*) reports to readers that current tariff policy threatens the plant because it enables foreign producers, with low wage rates, to undersell U.S. firms in domestic market.

In any large organization, the individual can easily begin to feel that he is lost in a sea of people. Sheer numbers may dull his feeling of personal accomplishment and suggest to him that he is a mere cog of no particular value or concern to leadership. In industry, the problem is intensified by the fact that the employee hears from all sides that he is lost sight of, that mass production techniques have smothered his individuality, and that his personal contribution to the enterprise goes unnoted and unappreciated.

Accordingly, the third major objective of any organization publication will be to give the individual a three-dimensional picture of the role he plays; to show that he has a respected and honorable place within his group, that he is valued as an individual, and that he can be proud of himself and his function. In industry, for example, the publication will point out that a company is merely an assembly of people and talents, and that its performance is the sum total of individual performances. It will show the enormous range of skills and special knowledge represented by a modern industrial operation, document the steady increase in skilled labor and show how the employee's mastery of new machines and technology has steadily expanded his output, opportunities, and living standards.

Examples of publication efforts to achieve such objectives are shown on following pages.

Responsibility of parents

REV. LOUIS J. PUTZ, C.S.C.

WE are generally aware of the responsibility parents have for the temporal welfare of the family, for keeping themselves and their children happy and healthy. What is less understood in this era of highly individualistic religion is the responsibility parents have for each other's spiritual welfare. Yet marriage is specially ordained to further supernatural development, because it is a sacrament, an external sign of an invisible grace that renders the recipients more fully one with Christ, more capable of fulfilling the vocation of parenthood, more filled with divine life and divine gifts.

Most of us understand that the priest is not the minister of the sacrament of marriage, but merely the official witness of the Church. It is do as husbands and wives, as fathers and mothers. That is why parents truly bless when they bless their children, when they instruct them in the ways of wisdom, when they help them and support them through the successive stages of their emotional and psychological, as well as physical, development.

Married people are not given the grace of state merely to carry out the functions of parenthood — this is something accomplished by every parent who is truly participating in God's creative power. But sacramental grace makes all the actions of parents grace-ful; they become bearers of grace to the recipients of their love and attention, provided that they act in the spirit of Christ and the Church. Parents are living a sacramental state, a consecrated state. They do not represent the Church to their children; they **are** the Church.

If this is true — and it is too bad that it is not preached more often from our pulpits and taught in our schools — then the problem of parents' responsibility for each other's

Church Publication

Student Responsibility in An Age of Challenge

~RAY FARABEE
President, USNSA

Eleven years ago delegates from more than 300 American colleges established the National Student Congress, based on the concept of responsible and democratic representation of campus opinion and dedicated to the development of student leadership in American higher education.

Each August since then students from all parts of the nation, from colleges and universities of every type and size, have met together to exchange ideas; discuss pertinent issues; develop programs; provide a voice for the American student community.

The need for full and enthusiastic student participation in such a meeting has never been more obvious than it is as we convene the 11th National Student Congress.

American education, forced into a frank if somewhat discouraging self-evaluation by events of the past year, is facing a crisis, the outcome of which is directly and irrevocably linked to the progress, even to the survival of civilization.

Students, as the members of the educational community most directly affected by change and by crisis, must assume a greater role in campus, national and international affairs.

Student Association

Opinion of Professional Ethics Committee

OPINION 292
(Adopted October 15, 1957)

COMPETITIVE BIDDING BY ATTORNEYS—The legal profession is a branch of the administration of justice, and the engagement of attorneys by a public agency or any other person seeking their services, as well as the amount of their fees for legal work, are not proper subjects of competitive bidding.

INDIRECT ADVERTISING—The effect of competitive bidding among lawyers for services to a governmental body, or other bodies or persons requiring legal services, results in indirect advertising and solicitation which is contrary to the Canons.

Canons 12, 27, 29
Opinion A. 83

The Grievance and Ethics Committee of a city bar association has requested a ruling in regard to the following situation:

"Representatives of the _____ _____ School Board have contacted several attorneys and firms of attorneys in _____, with the request that the School Board be given a firm figure for handling the following legal work:

represent the School Board for a stated period of time.

Attorneys in the area who were contacted questioned the procedure of the School Board on the belief that it would result in competitive bidding amongst local attorneys. They argued that such procedure would ultimately be detrimental to the public interest since it would not take into account the normal personal relationship between client and attorney, nor would it take into consideration the true worth of the

Professional Journal

Higher Slots to Go To 'Best - Qualified'

With the receipt of Second Army Memorandum 624-1, commanders in the area will consider educational qualifications when selecting soldiers for promotions to grades E-4 through E-9. Second Army is endeavoring to improve the quality of the individual and the same time to insure that the "best qualified" are promoted.

Those with such desired attributes as exemplary combat and leadership records, but cannot be validated with high school equivalency, will not necessarily be barred from promotion.

Prior to promotion, personnel should be able to satisfy the following requirements for academic achievement:

● **Promotion to E-4**—Personnel records must show eighth grade or satisfactory completion of Preparatory Instruction.

● **Promotion to E-5, E-6, and E-7**—In addition to satisfying prerequisites established for grade E-4, individuals whose personnel records do not show high school education or GED equivalent will be required to take the high-school level GED test. Appointing authorities will consider

Military Newspaper

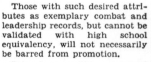

How nonindustrial organizations relate members to their role and function is suggested by the clippings above. A church informs its members that, as parents, they are responsible for the temporal and moral welfare of their families. The student newspaper reminds members that their participation determines the association's effectiveness. The professional journal reviews ethical principles which members are expected to observe, while the Army publication points out that the best qualified soldiers will receive promotions.

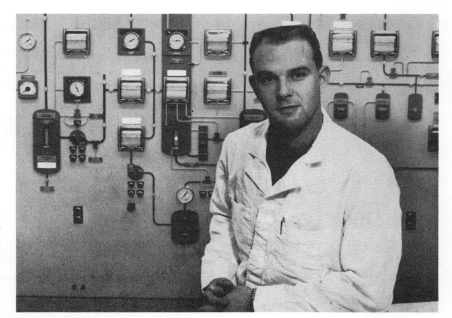

➤ **CAREER SPECIALIST** at Antioch Works is man like 24-year-old Control Operator Dayton Jennings, a former mail carrier who now handles complex chemical operations in a large tetraethyl lead unit from central control room. He is counterpart of hundreds of Du Pont control operators throughout company.

CAREER SPECIALIST: Chemical Operator's Job Shows Responsibilities, Prestige and Rewards Now Found in Industry

A big change is underway in industry. Symbolized in the chemical flask image, left, it is personal in nature, quiet in its upheavals, but persistent in its progress.

The change is told in the jobs of men like Dayton Jennings, above, an employee at Du Pont's new Antioch Works in California. Once a new employee in industry was hired largely for his strength and brawn. Now, non-muscular know-how and intelligence assume new significance. For as industrial sociologists

CAREER MAN'S PLANT is outdoor maze of multi-level piping, chemical stills and process tanks, interconnected to run on a continuous basis.

point out, the average worker is exercising an ever-increasing measure of selectivity, judgment and mental application in his everyday responsibilities.

While some people worry lest today's trend toward mechanized and instrumented plants may ultimately reduce the importance of the individual, the facts show the reverse. At Antioch, Jennings and 350 other Du Pont employees have started up a large new plant for tetraethyl lead and "Freon" refrigerants. Already, they have shared in a $1.3 million training and start-up program. In the process, Jennings and his associates have mastered new skills, acquired new knowledge and enlarged their career possibilities. Rather than losing personal identity, a man like Jennings actually has achieved new measures of dignity. His is the responsibility, shared eight hours a day with his 11-man shift, of operating a vast, complex chemical plant. Generally $35,000 or more is invested in each job at a new plant like this. At Jennings' fingertips are 200 finely calibrated instruments that keep in

balance the process that turns lead, sodium, and ethyl chloride into tetraethyl lead, a key additive of gasoline. In theory, automatic instruments keep the plant running smoothly; in practice, the human element is vital. It is employed at a higher degree of skill than ever.

No period in history has witnessed such a significant rise in the job status of the working man. Modern industry presents new opportunities for self-development denied to earlier generations.

CAREER MAN'S SHIFT at Antioch is team of 11 carefully-trained men,* whose skills must be coordinated to operate the intricate TEL process.

A basic problem in any organization is to preserve the individual's feeling of personal responsibility and worth, his conviction that he plays a useful and productive role in the organization and in society. Building the employee's pride in himself and enlarging his awareness of the important personal contribution he makes to the organization is a task that a company publication can perform with great effectiveness. In the story reprinted here, "Career Specialist," the editor points out that today the traits in demand are not strength and brawn but "nonmuscular know-how and intelligence." The trend toward mechanized and instrumented plants has increased the importance of the individual; the operator's responsibilities, skills, personal status, prestige, and rewards have grown, and he enjoys "opportunities for self-development denied to earlier generations."

A is for Accountant Phil Comer, Treasurer's Dept. Also: acid wringer, air tool operator, analyst, animal caretaker and auditor.

B is for Blacksmith John Chodkiewicz of the Parlin F & F plant. Also: baker, biologist, boiler operator, brakeman, bricklayer and butcher.

C is for Chemist Henry Miller, Chemical Dept. Also: cabinetmaker, cake wrapper, carpenter, cashier, clerk, coater and coppersmith.

D is for Draftsman Henry Falcon, Engineering Dept. Also: delooper, designer, die maker, dispatcher and dope house operator

I is for Instrument Mechanic Bill Coman, Parlin Photo Products. Also: impregnator, ingredient tester, inspector, insulator and ironworker.

J is for Jitney Operator Edward Jamison of the Carney's Point Explosives plant. Also: janitor, jet perforator operator and jig operator.

K is for Knitter Albert Johnson, Carothers Research Laboratory. Also: kettle charger, knife set-up man and kneader operator.

L is for Leadburner John Davis, Chambers Works. Also: labeler, laboratory technician, laborer, lift truck operator, librarian and lineman.

Q is for Quality Control Operator Ethel Kovacs of Buffalo Film Test Laboratory, who checks coated cellophane.

R is for Rigger George Conner, Chambers Works. Also: reel cutter, refrigerator engineer, reject collector, rivet operator and roofer.

S is for Secretary Evelyn Hurley, Chambers Works. Also: sandblaster, salesman, shader, spinner, storekeeper, splicer, supervisor and stripper.

T is for Telephone Operator Rose Stigliano of Wilmington offices. Also: tinsmith, toolmaker, truck driver, transitman, tunnelman and typist.

"C" IS FOR CORPORATION

Industry's Alphabet Is Spelled Out by People Whose Talents, Skills and Experiences Are the Heart and Soul of a Business Like Du Pont

A gray, stone-faced edifice on Wall Street, a shining skyscraper in mid-Manhattan, a name on a frosty office door — that is the picture conjured up in the minds of most people when the word "corporation" is mentioned.

A corporation, actually, is none of these. Offices, signs, and even plants and laboratories are but the visible evidences of an industrial corporation's existence. Basically, a corporation is people. Webster defines it as "a body of persons united for a common purpose." Thus a corporation may be a charitable, religious or fraternal organization. Or it may be a business.

A corporation like Du Pont is simply an organization of people who have united in the common purpose of making a

Dispelling the illusion that "the company" or "the corporation" is an abstract and soul-less entity, and emphasizing that it has no existence apart from people will be a prime task of the well-conceived employee publication. In this article, the editor has chosen the simple device of the alphabet to feature a few of the countless individuals whose talents, skills, and abilities combine to make up the team known as a corporation. Adding his skills to the pool represented by

E is for Electrician Fred Norris of Wilmington Shops. Also: economist, elevator operator, engineer, "Erifon" operator and estimator.

F is for Foreman Carl Gilmore, Chambers Works. Also: field project manager, filler, fireman, floorman, formaldehyde operator and formulator.

G is for Glassblower Dave Myers of Chemical Dept. Also: gardener, geologist, gluer, glycerin handler, gauger and grinder operator.

H is for Hydrolysis Operator Horace Johnson of Edge Moor plant. Also: heat treater, helper and hydrostat test operator.

M is for Manager Martin Valentine, Carney's Point. Also: machinist, mason, mechanic, messenger, mill operator and meterman.

N is for Nurse Arlene Woolley, Parlin F&F plant. Also: nailing machine operator, neutralizer operator, nickeler and nitrator operator.

O is for Oiler Norman Kreismer, Parlin Photo Products plant. Also: offset platemaker, oil well shooter, "Ozalid" operator, overcoater.

P is for Pressman Harry Palmer, at Philadelphia Printing Plant. Also: painter, photographer, plater, pot still operator and proofreader.

U is for Upholsterer Amos Bryant of Office Buildings Dept. Also: uniformity inspector, uptwist operator, unloader and utility mechanic.

V is for Valve Repairman John Puckett of Chambers Works. Also: varnish cooker, varnish pretester, vacuum crystalizer and viscosity man.

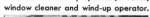

W is for Welder Joseph La Joie, Carney's Point. Also: waste recovery operator, weaver, window cleaner and wind-up operator.

X is for X-Ray Roll Stock Inspector Doris Siemon, Parlin Photo Products. Also: Xerox operator, x-ray packer, x-ray technician.

living by producing the best possible products at the lowest price consistent with quality and service.

The "body of persons" in a large corporation embraces a wide variety of skills and talents. Altogether, Du Pont now has more than 103,000 employees including: 66,000 who man plants in 25 states; 5,000 engaged in research and development; 22,000 who are building new plants and facilities for the company and the government; and 10,000 other employees including those in offices from Yakima, Wash., to Jacksonville, Fla.

Classified according to their training, experience and talent, these men and women represent Du Pont alphabets which, like the pictures on these and the following pages, really spell out a corporation like E. I. du Pont de Nemours & Co. (Inc.).

Y is for Yardman Henry Fones, Chemical Dept. Also: yard pumpman, yardmaster, yarn machine operator and yarn purification operator.

Z is for Zoologist Duncan Sells, Grasselli Chemicals Dept., who works with Florida ranchers. Also: zinc chloride diluter and zinc plater.

such a group, the individual is enabled to achieve far greater and more significant feats than he could by working alone. Often editors vary such a feature as this by showing the many kinds of scientists required to conduct a rounded research program, or the host of engineering specialties called upon to design and build a plant.

WALTER DURHAM, operator at Du Pont's Richmond, Va., cellophane plant, reflects in his experiences the opportunities and environment in a modern corporation. Now 34, he has been with Du Pont 12 years.

THE UPGRADED WORKER

His skills and status climb with industrial progress

The most direct insight into life in a large corporation is perhaps provided by the jobs and personal experiences of the employees in its production arm. They are the largest single group in industry, and the most obvious beneficiaries of the technological progress that has made U.S. corporations the most productive in the world. Walter Durham, pictured on these pages, is one of about 45,000 production workers in Du Pont.

As a corporation, Du Pont can provide him facilities to produce that he could not obtain individually. Backed by a prodigious investment, he is able to produce, in an eight-hour day, 10 times as much as a workman using the tools and techniques of the 19th Century. Because his productivity is high, his living standard is high.

The corporation entrusts him with a high degree of responsibility. An error on his part can disrupt the carefully scheduled flow of work through a plant employing more than 1000 people, and a maximum of skill and judgment thus is inherent in his job.

By the nature of its work, the corporation must ask that he work an unusual schedule involving rotating shifts. But when the need for this is understood, he has found it easy to adapt himself to it.

BETTER JOBS: More opportunities for skilled workers broaden job horizons

14%	CLERICAL WORKERS	26%
50%	UNSKILLED WORKERS	24%
36%	SKILLED WORKERS	50%

1910 ········ 1956

UPGRADED SKILLS of today's U.S. workers are reflected in chart showing the trend away from unskilled labor.

Your Know-How
Large and Growing, It Is A Prime Competitive Asset

In ancient times, it was not at all impossible for one man —like Aristotle—to know just about everything there was to know. With the development of modern science and technology, however, the body of human knowledge became far too vast to be contained by a single head. People became specialists—experts in specific subjects and types of work.

Nowhere is this more evident than in industry; today more than 80 per cent of all industrial workers have skilled and semi-skilled jobs, and the number is growing. But statistics tell only part of the story of a complex plant like Louisville Works: Today, a typical plant employee has an intimate knowledge of processes and techniques which were unknown even a few decades ago. With average Du Pont operating investment running at $26,900 per employee, he is frequently responsible for the efficient operation of more equipment than a Civil War general. A maximum of skill, knowledge, and judgment is inherent in his job.

Thus, what we call "Louisville Works know-how" is a body of knowledge made up of hundreds of employee specialties ranging from the testing of insulation on electric motors to sending finished neoprene on its way to waiting customers. A cross-section of plant jobs — and the kinds of employee knowledge and talent they represent—is shown here.

KNOW-HOW: PRODUCTION — R. T. "Tommy" Lowe, "Freon" Products Area, typical of chemical operators throughout the chemical industry, although he has modern instrumentation to help insure safe operation, product quality and low production cost, still holds one of the most responsible manufacturing jobs at Louisville Works. He must understand the operation of thousands of dollars worth of equipment and keep it running perfectly, keeping a sharp look out for any quality deviation.

KNOW-HOW: ELECTRICAL — Electrician Ed Dietz brings to the plant's know-how a knowledge of electrical wiring, circuits and motors, buttressed by 15 years' experience keeping power flowing to plant areas. Ed helps maintain many motors and electrical devices developed to improve quality. Above he makes insulation test of winding on 75 h.p. well motor.

KNOW-HOW: INSTRUMENTS — Instrument mechanic, Aubrey Pierce, shown repairing potentiometer which records temperature in a process stream, is one of the instrument specialists who share responsibility for maintaining intricate instruments and controls at Louisville Works. His know-how comes from training and experience. He has 17 years of Du Pont service.

KNOW-HOW: SHIPPING — Jeppie Green, former lift fork operator recently promoted to shift leader, brings his 15 years of know-how and experience into daily use as he helps fill our customers' orders for neoprene. Besides bringing right type of product to shipping pla form, Jeppie also relocates stock to provide extra space, beter identification.

In 50 years, industrial progress has more than halved the number of unskilled workers; skilled and clerical workers now comprise about three fourths of the total U.S. work force. The industrial editor will want repeatedly to depict this important change, showing that multiplying job skills have enhanced the employee's personal status, responsibilities, rewards, and pride in himself. In the articles above, the editors have focused upon "upgraded skills" and "job know-how," pointing out that the modern worker has an intimate knowledge of processes and techniques which were unheard of even a few years ago; the individual's job has changed from one of largely physical labor to one in which a maximum of skill, knowledge, and responsibility are inherent.

Our Plant: A Giant Tool Box

Few Of Today's Skilled Workers Could Carry — Or Buy — Their Own Tools

Time was when the trademark of the skilled craftsman was a well-stocked, tool box like the carpenter's chest displayed (top right) by Carpenter Charlie Morris, Project Group. Such a set of personal tools was carefully chosen and closely guarded, for the craftsman knew that the working partnership of his skills and his tools was his best guarantee of good wages and steady employment.

But you don't have to walk through many areas on this Plant to see how the situation has changed. For modern industrial processes like ours have come to require the use of machines and tools of giant size and giant cost—far beyond the means of any employee. In DuPont today, for example, investment in plant tools and working capital per employee averages $25,200. Often, the equipment is designed for only one job on one plant. Many of these expensive tools are soon outmoded and must be modified or replaced. But expensive as they are, they make the present day skilled worker far more productive than any craftsman of the past.

Only one source can supply the immense amount of money needed to buy the costly tools of modern American industry: the savings of the American people. Through the investment of these savings, such equipment as the machines and tools demonstrated on this page by typical DuPont employees can be teamed with employee skills to turn out more products of higher quality. One of the critical factors in American society today is the maintenance of an economic climate that will provide incentives for savings and investments—for the means to build the large tool boxes on which rising living standards depend.

TOOL CHEST Charlie Morris, Carpenter, Project Group, is shown with his locker of personal tools necessary to performance of his job. In comparison, tools needed in modern industry is beyond employee's purchasing power. DuPont's investment is $25,200 per employee.

LABORATORY EQUIPMENT needed for testing or research, as in the analysis being run here by Chemist Harry Brazzell, calls for especially precise, delicate — and expensive — materials. This Spectrophotometer alone costs $8000. Because these tools are fine and precise, they make it possible to detect the slightest deviations from our top quality standards, and help make certain the product we make will continue to satisfy our customers.

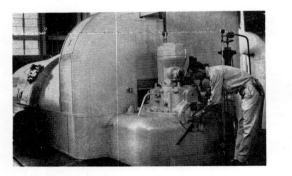

POWER EQUIPMENT like the turbine tended by Power Operator John Booth, "D" Shift, requires an investment of approximately $1,000,000 each. (We have 3 turbines in the Powerhouse.) This hugh source of energy is able to send 10,000 horsepower (per turbine) surging through the Plant's circuits night and day to supply our needs.

To demonstrate that modern machines and processes enhance the employee's output and rewards, a publication should frequently run features that dramatize the way technology has revolutionized the nature of work. Backed by a prodigious investment, the modern employee is able to produce in an eight-hour day 10 times as much as a workman using the tools and techniques of the nineteenth century. The result: because his productivity is high, his living standard is also high. Feature above (left) makes this point in an interesting way by likening a plant to a giant tool box, whose investment in tools per employee is $25,000. Article (right) reports the vast stores of mechanical energy put at the

DRILLING: Using only enough of his own power to move lever on this drill press, Stanley releases energy of 70 men to bore three-inch hole through hard steel. Drill is powered by 7½ horsepower motor.

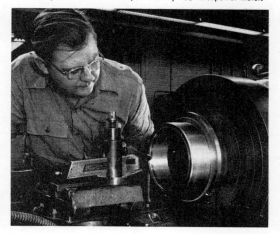

TURNING: Stanley has the strength of 70 men after he presses the motor button on his engine lathe. With this added power he easily whittles out 10-foot-long blocks of hard metal into precise shapes.

LIFTING: It would take combined effort of 640 men to equal the power of this 20-ton bridge crane as it lifts casting from Stanley Lutcavage's engine lathe at Wilmington Shops.

OPERATOR COMMANDS IN MECHANICAL ENERGY THE STRENGTH OF 236 MEN

The touch of a button gives Stanley Lutcavage, Wilmington Shops machine operator, the average added strength of 236 men. On special tasks (above) he may use more. Hand-grinding of metal, laborious drilling, back-bending lifting of work in progress—these burdensome tasks have been taken over by mechanical energy in the modern industrial operation. Stanley on his job and his wife at home (see next page) have as their servants a vast array of useful tools for which they supply only the direction. Electricity or the internal combustion engine furnish power.

In Stanley's great-grandfather's time, the industrial employee worked an average of 77 hours a week in an industrial plant. He had few power tools to help him on the job, and it took him that long to earn a subsistence wage. Today, by contrast, Stanley works about half as long to produce five times as much at five times the pay. Such is the individual's share in the bounty of goods and leisure created by technology's advances.

GRINDING: It would take Stanley and Grinder Operator Russell Howe five hours of hard labor to equal the work performed in five minutes by this big cylindrical grinder as it smooths a nylon feeder spool.

average operator's disposal by the introduction of machines—energy equivalent to the strength of 236 human helpers. Compared to his counterpart of a century ago, the individual today works half as long to produce five times as much at fives times the pay.

EIGHT SONS return to visit their father, Charles Eaton (third from left), on his 112-acre farm near Rockport, W. Va. Not one of his sons is a farmer or intends to be one. One son, Paul (below and fifth from left, above), is an operator at Du Pont's Washington, W. Va., Works. His brothers are an auto mechanic, a crane operator, a minister, a hardware clerk, an industrial mechanic, a truck driver, a high-school student who wants to be an engineer.

FREEDOM OF OPPORTUNITY

Survey Shows U. S. Youths Choose Their Own Careers, Are No Longer Restricted by Family Background or Parental Example

One of the extraordinary but often unappreciated aspects of U.S. society today is the degree of freedom the individual enjoys in choosing his life work. At Du Pont's plant near Parkersburg, W. Va., for example, a BETTER LIVING survey reveals that 87.9 per cent of the employees are not following in their fathers' work (neither, as a matter of fact, are 85.9 per cent of the employees' brothers). Almost two-thirds of the fathers are, or were, employed in non-manufacturing work, and only 12.1 per cent are in the chemical industry, including glass manufacturing. Among non-manufacturing professions, merchants and small businessmen provide this Du Pont unit with the most offspring, followed closely by farmers and mechanics.

This pattern contrasts sharply with that of Colonial America, and even with the experience of many European youths today. Freedom of op-

AT DU PONT for last six years, Paul Eaton (shown at top with his brothers and father) is a tapered bristle operator at the Washington Works.

portunity to pursue careers other than those predetermined by family background or parental example is a comparatively recent development. The individual is no longer bound and restricted, in the European sense, to a specific trade. Rather, science and industry have so broadened his opportunities that family background or parental choice is no more the major factor in career selection. Today, any youngster, given the ability, determination, and education, can aim for almost any kind of job — and usually get it.

Those who would picture modern industrial society as restrictive on the individual, or unresponsive to his needs, overlook or ignore the barriers that have been flattened by broader education, a diversity of new and more productive jobs, and elevation of living standards. Family background and economic status no longer keep talented youngsters from moving into new fields.

The emergence of a highly productive industrial economy has brought many revolutionary improvements in living patterns—improvements that are often unnoticed and unappreciated. Employee publications can perform solid service by developing their readers' perspective and awareness of the vast social, economic, and vocational progress made by the individual under industrial institutions. One example of such an important change is "mobility of occupation"; science, technology and the scale of modern business institutions have freed the individual

RE·VERITEZ·DV·SIECLE·DAPRESENT·

RESTRICTION ON CLOTHING affected every class of medieval society. Custom and occupation determined the kinds of clothes one wore. Peasants, for instance, were forbidden to wear the ornaments, decorations, jewelry or wigs of the nobility under penalty of dire punishment. And the nobility was equally hamstrung: Each noble garment, wig, lace, or shoe was carefully prescribed, and deviations from these royal directives often meant banishment from the court. This restrictive attitude extended to the clergy's clothing style, which in certain orders comes down to modern times unchanged.

FEUDAL LIFE WAS A VAST PRISON

Jean Roget, a young man of 20 living in Belgium three centuries ago, might have been an apprentice or a farm hand. That depended usually on what his father was. But the restrictions on his life and his opportunities did not stop there. Like all people in those days, Jean had a set place in society —to which he was born and from which he never moved. He wore the clothes of his class, married in his class, ate the food of his class, died and was buried like them. Some restrictions that bound Jean and other young men are shown on these pages.

The plight of Jean Roget seems ridiculous to young men today. To them, it is incomprehensible that the individual ever should have been so circumscribed, not alone in his career but in so many other areas. The freedoms and opportunities taken for granted today are, historically, comparatively recent. Only when industrialism burst the confining walls of feudalism did man find a way to improve his material and spiritual circumstance and broaden his opportunities.

RESTRICTION ON TRADE extended to all commerce. Cloth, for instance, was restricted as to amount, quality, price, imports and exports. Prices and styles were geared only to the very rich townspeople and nobility. Peasants never shopped in stores. All shops were in one location so government and merchants' guilds could keep exact and forbidding eye on commercial transactions and control them.

RESTRICTION ON PROFESSION was universal. A youngster's occupation was selected from birth: he followed in his father's footsteps or he entered the clergy. If his father was an engraver, above, so was the son. Each profession had restrictions as to length of apprenticeship and amount of production. No one could move out of his field of work or rise above it.

from ancient family, geographical, class and social restrictions; a youth may choose any career he likes and go as high and far as his abilities will take him. Article reprinted here makes this point interestingly by surveying plant population and finding that 87 per cent of employees are in occupations different than those of their fathers; the editor features one family whose eight sons chose eight different occupations, ranging from auto mechanic and industrial worker to clergyman and engineer.

Objective Number 4: BUILDING PARTICIPATION IN THOSE ACTIVITIES THAT IMPROVE THE ORGANIZATION'S EFFICIENCY AND EFFECTIVENESS

The three publication objectives earlier described have aimed to lay the foundation for an effective organization by building the individual's pride in, and understanding of, his institution and his own role within it. The fourth objective calls upon the individual for co-operation and personal action that will enable the organization to operate with maximum efficiency.

In reaching this goal, the employee publication will cover a host of pressing plant and company concerns. For example, typical features will solicit the individual's participation in cost-reduction or conservation campaigns and request his aid in producing a quality product. Likewise, the periodical will persuade the employee to work safely, to follow standard practices, to maintain good housekeeping, and to suggest ways by which his area can perform its function with greater effectiveness.

A sampling of publication efforts to achieve such objectives is shown on the following pages.

Bishop Asks Faithful to Assume Responsibility on Schools, Movies

STEUBENVILLE, Ohio (NC). —Bishop John King Mussio of Steubenville has called on Catholics to "assume their personal responsibility" in modern society, especially in the fields of education and entertainment.

In a pastoral letter Bishop Mussio reminded the faithful that "no one grows up in the true sense of the word, either spiritually or physically, unless he assumes the obligations of his maturity."

The Bishop first called on Catholic parents to "assume their personal responsibility in the proper education of their children."

"Parents must grow up too," he said, "and this growing up is found in their matching the efforts of the Church to train their children in the love and fear of God."

The Bishop called on Catholics to show mature responsibility in their attitude toward the motion picture industry which, he charged, has taken to presenting immorality and brutality as "a policy of desperation" aimed to "jack up falling box office receipts."

"You must make sure there is no doubt in the minds of your local theatre managers just where you stand on the subject of indecent shows," he said.

"If the manager won't listen to your appeal for decent movies, he will be forced to listen to the money jingling in your pocket rather than in his till."

Bishop Mussio also pointed out that "unless the movie industry is ready to accept its personal responsibility to the good order of the community, the movie house itself is doomed to become an anachronism mentioned to the children of tomorrow as a quaint old habit of yore."

November Installation For Chicago Archbishop

MILWAUKEE (NC). — The representative of His Holiness Pope Pius XII to the Church in the United States will install Archbishop Albert G. Meyer of Milwaukee as the new Archbishop of Chicago at an as yet undetermined date in mid-November.

His Excellency Archbishop Amleto Giovanni Cicognani, the Apostolic Delegate, will preside at the installation in Holy Name Cathedral, Chicago, it was announced here.

Archbishop Meyer, at 55 the

Church Periodical

Announce Dress Regulations For NCO Club Members Here

The Board of Governors of the newly renovated Meade Noncommissioned Officers' Open Mess has announced the following dress regulations to be observed by NCO club members. These rules, according to the board, were designed so as not to limit the enjoyment of members but to insure the decorum of members and their guests.

Included in the dress regulations are:

• Unless otherwise outlined, members will dress in the manner prescribed by current uniform regulations of this installation.

• Clothing, civilian or military, will always be clean, neat and in a generally presentable condition.

• Shirts will always be worn tucked inside of trousers; this is to include sport-type shirts.

• Ties will be worn with uniform after 6 p.m. Ties will be worn with dress shirts at all be worn by female members or guests after 6 p.m.

• No blue-jeans will be worn at anytime.

• Slacks or pedal-pushers will not be worn by female members or guests after 6 p.m. No slacks or pedal-pushers on Sundays or holidays.

• Shorts will not be worn by female members or guests at any time.

• Shorts for male members will not be worn at any time, except the abbreviated uniform and then post uniform regulations will apply.

• Athletic jackets or any jackets with emblems and fancy designs will not be worn at any time.

• On special nights, the dress will be appropriate to the occasion as announced.

• On dance nights a coat will be worn with either a sport shirt or dress shirt.

Military Newspaper

Here's How to Help Yourself To Easier, Faster Road Service

With Keystone Automobile Club prepared to give more efficient Emergency Road Service than ever this Winter, you can help yourself secure this service easily and rapidly by following the few pointers below:

Be prepared! Before you call for service have this information handy: Your membership number, your license number (why not write it down, right now, on your membership card?), your car's exact location, the symptoms leading to your difficulty.

When you call state to our operator **and** dispatcher that you want Emergency Road Service. Our dispatchers will then want to know your name and your membership number.

Where is your car? These items help us speed service by "pin pointing" your location: (a) The street and house number where your car is located, or the street your car is on plus the name of the nearest intersecting street. (b) The make year and body style of your car helps our mechanic spot your car from a distance. (c) The license number serves as his final check on whether he is at the right car.

Where are you? You should stay with the car when possible, but with the number of the phone you used when you placed the call, we can keep in touch with you if unexpected (and, thank goodness, infrequent) delays to service should occur.

What's the trouble? Your service will be faster and the service truck free for the next call sooner, if the mechanic can prepare for your car in advance. Battery dead? He'll bring a "booster." In an accident? He'll use a tow truck rather than a service car.

By using the above pointers you can help yourself to better service —and help us in rendering it more efficiently and effectively. Why not

Automobile Club

Clippings above indicate how nonbusiness organizations invite their members' active aid and support in reaching desired goals. The religious body urges its people to assume personal responsibility for protecting the young from undesirable motion pictures. The Army newspaper requests personnel to observe uniform regulations. The automobile club asks members to follow prescribed procedures in requesting emergency service.

Mix-Control

Proper Product Segregation and Identification are Vital Part of Quality for Customer Satisfaction

Too much emphasis cannot be placed on the importance of following our mix-control procedures, for there is no mistaking the fact that the security of our business depends upon the proper segregation, identification, and quality of our product. We must realize that our jobs depend upon customer satisfaction.

If one of our customers receives our product containing a mix, it can mean that he will have loss of production time or second grade fabric—or both. However, it *will* mean that our customer will lose confidence and faith in our ability to supply him with top grade quality, constantly. Let's not overlook the prime fact that our customer is in business to make a profit. He has too many headaches from production and competitive problems in his own bailiwick to tolerate other than top quality, mix-free nylon from us. There are other manufacturers of synthetic fibers.

Customer and consumer demands are causing a radical change in the textile market. In the near future, we may expect to handle a large volume of small orders in numerous "counts". Our segregation and identification procedures, if followed minutely, are our best guarantee for customer satisfaction.

1 Glenn Hamstead, "B" Shift, Spinning. checks empty bobbins for removal of any identification insignia of nylon formerly on bobbins. Glenn knows value of mix-control procedures to customer satisfaction.

2 Elsie Evans, "A" Shift, Textile, leaves no stone unturned in checking every package of nylon, that passes through her hands, for proper identification. One wrong pirn can cause untold damage to the customer.

3 Every area has many mix-control procedures—each highly important. Here in Staple, Earl Anthony, "A" Shift, checks label on each bale, as bale is weighed, with recorded information in area's log book.

5 Edward Melvin, "A" Shift, Beaming, knows that DuPont is in business for a profit and that there isn't any profit in shipping the wrong beam construction to a customer and incurring his dissatisfaction. Mix-control procedures check proper ends, weight, type.

Enlisting employee aid in solving quality, production, or process problems is an area in which a well-planned publication can do an outstanding job. Basically, most stories of this type will stress the importance of quality workmanship in pleasing the customer; for example, many editors will trace a unit of product through customer mills, or will produce a picture story following a company salesman as he makes his rounds. Other features will have a sharp focus on specific production problems or quality defects which must be eliminated. The story reprinted here discusses the serious problems created by product "mixes," and it urges readers to follow standard operating procedures so that only the best product goes to the plant's boss, the customer.

Cost Reduction....
through Improved Yields

R. A. Hrabe, Plant Manager, recently keynoted our cost reduction program by emphasizing the fact that there are a number of ways to reach and maintain our objective—all of which we must ultimately take to keep DuPont nylon abreast of other competitive fibers. "Right now," Mr. Hrabe stated, "is the time to start reducing the cost of our operations by improving our yields. This requires that all of us do a real 'watchmaker's job' by exercising, fully, our abilities and job know-how. Beyond a doubt, we can do it! We need improvement and we have the means to fulfill this need. Let's exercise these means and put our product on top and keep it there," he concluded.

The textile fibers business, including the manufacture of nylon, is a highly competitive field. Customers will buy DuPont nylon only if they feel it will do a better job, than any of the other many fibers, in creating end products attractive to consumers and profitable to the manufacturers.

Our customers, and in turn their customers, are constantly searching for merchandise of increasingly better quality at increasingly lower prices. In order to maintain our business, we must meet competition by keeping our customers satisfied. This means we must reduce the cost of producing nylon to a minimum in order to offer DuPont nylon at the right prices for volume production and profitable operations. This is the reason for our Plant's cost reduction program aimed at eliminating all unnecessary expenses.

The job of reducing costs is an overall important factor in our job security. There is no need for pessimism about the future of our product, but we must be realistic about the job each of us has to do.

PROPER BALANCE in not being too conservative or too liberal, when inspecting our product, is most essential in reducing costs through improving yields. Catherine Trice, "D" Shift, Textile, adheres to standard practice— she has all questionable yarn checked before making any disposition.

ABILITY and know-how of the man on the job is the most important tool in helping to reduce our costs through improved yields. All have the ability and know-how. It remains for each of us to use them 1440 minutes each working day. Using our know-how full time will help keep DuPont nylon on top.

REVIEW Ken Winston and Dick Otwell, "D" Shift, P & S, like many others, make a practice of reviewing standard practices and procedures periodically. This is done to prevent any oversight or "drifting away" from any small detail that could lower our yields and increase our costs.

IMPROVEMENTS Improved equipment and modification are under constant study by Process and Technical Groups to add their share to increased yields and quality. (Kim von Storch, Process, checks blueprint.) Improvement will aid, but not equal job know-how in reducing costs.

EXTRA EYES Jim Anthony, Process Checker, is one of several extra pairs of eyes that assist operators by making a double check of all processes. This helps to insure quick detection of any off-standard conditions—thus improving yields, reducing costs; both of which promote job security.

Every firm tries to maintain customer favor by providing products of increasingly higher quality at increasingly lower prices. Thus, in every enterprise, it is essential that management enlist employee efforts to reduce waste, conserve ma-

That Is The $64,000 Question

Gloves – $43,541.00

Wiping Rags – $7,663.00

Flashlights – $2,757.00
Flashlight Batteries – $2,525.00

Shown on this page are a few of the hundreds of items used on the plant during the immediate past twelve months, together with their cost. The total of these items is $64,000. The nine items selected merely represent a sampling of the many little costs of producing our two products—neoprene and "Freon-22" monochlorodifluoromethane.

Suppose you did pay these bills during the past twelve months; would your use of them have changed? That is the big $64,000 question!

Here are the items selected and the tab picked up by the plant for our use of each last year. The Inventory Control Group furnished the cost figures of all the items pictured on this page.

GLOVES	$43,541.00
WIPING RAGS	7,663.00
FLASHLIGHTS	2,757.00
FLASHLIGHT BATTERIES	2,525.00
ENVELOPES	2,381.00
SOAP	2,286.00
PAPER TOWELS	1,650.00
LENS TISSUE	806.00
TWINE	391.00
GRAND TOTAL	$64,000.00

In addition to the above items, which total $64,000, the Power Division gives us another. In less than six days, Power Division supervision tells us, we use on this plant $64,000 worth of power—electricity, water and steam!

Perhaps it would be better if each of us, rather than attempting to answer our $64,000 question, would ask himself another question—a fairly simple and yet a completely logical one. "How can I help reduce costs?"

How Can We Reduce Costs?

Here are some of the ways each employee can help to reduce costs: (1) Follow standard procedures on every job; (2) Take good care of all tools and equipment; (3) Don't waste anything—time, effort or materials; and (4) Suggest ways to reduce costs on your job.

Here, also, are some simple rules it would be well for each of us to remember: Do not order more items than are needed; return all excess items; plan your job to make full use of all materials; make that little extra effort to cut down costs. It could mean the difference between our having or not having a job in today's highly competitive chemical industry. Savings that can be made in our material costs will reflect directly on our competitive position in the industry.

The reduction of costs means job security. By watching the nickels and dimes, we can save dollars! The answer to this big question and the other big $64,000 question pertaining to the conservation of materials and cost reduction lies with each of us. From October 1, 1955, to September 30, 1956, the items shown on this page cost exactly $64,000. For this period, this represents about thirty dollars per employee.

Soap – $2,286.00

Paper Towels – $1,650.00

Lens Tissue – $806.00

terials and keep production costs down to the lowest possible levels. Two interesting stories calling for employee aid in this realm are reprinted above. The article (*left*) attracts reader attention by quoting the top authority, the plant manager, who asks employees to cut costs by applying all their experience and know-how to the job of improving yields in every phase of the production process. Feature (*right*) calls for employee co-operation in eliminating waste of operating supplies. Editor cites cross section of items whose combined annual cost of $64,000 can be sharply reduced if employees intensify their conservation efforts. Companies usually find such stories as these highly effective if they are specific, cite concrete examples, and tell employees exactly what they can do to help in solving the problem.

Your Hot Ideas Are Worth Cold Cash

SURE I WILL VOTE IN THE NLRB ELECTION NEXT WEEK. I AM GLAD TO HAVE A CHANCE TO VOTE FOR WHAT I THINK IS RIGHT.

VOTING SCHEDULE

WEDNESDAY ⎱ 5:00 a.m.-11:00 a.m.
October 8 ⎰ 3:00 p.m.- 6:30 p.m.
THURSDAY ⎱ 7:00 a.m.-9:00 a.m.
October 9 ⎰ 3:00 p.m.-6:30 p.m.

ALL VOTING WILL TAKE PLACE IN THE FACTORY CONFERENCE ROOMS

Cooper Urges Full Vote

Plant Manager E. M. Cooper, Jr. urges that every eligible employee cast a vote in the representation election to be held on October 8 and 9.

"The issue confronting the employees of this plant is a very important one to all concerned," Mr. Cooper stated. "Only by the exercise of the right to vote can the will of the majority be determined.

"It is my hope that every eligible employee will cast a

Suggestion Program Disbursed $274,423

The Suggestion Award Program will mark its fourth anniversary in January.

While no plans are being made for an elaborate cake cutting ceremony, it is felt that the occasion can best be used to review the plan.

In the course of its operation to date a total of 18,552 suggestions have been received, while 6794 awards were made. The ideas netted plant employees a handsome $274,423 which has been used for everything from taking "the little woman" to dinner to buying home workshop power tools, outboard motors, sporting equipment and household appliances.

The Suggestion Award Program is under the guidance of the Cost Reduction Section of the Control Department. H. F. Malzeke, head of this Section, urged everyone to look around and try to discover some improvement that can be made. Even those who have already reaped the benefits of being observant are eligible for another try. Some suggestors have been paid off for many different ideas.

No one is more cognizaant of possible improvements than the individual actually on the particular job. Realizing this, the Company hopes that both the employee and it will be able to profit from this fact.

phase of it. Be sure that it is feasible and that an actual saving in time, money, or effort will be realized. Then start working out the mechanics of it. Anyone in your supervision will be more than willing to work the details out with you.

When the Improvement Suggestion Form (available in all area offices) has been filled out, then give it to your supervision. From there it will be sent to the Suggestion Office. Here it will be stamped with the date received and a number will be assigned to it. From this same office will be sent to you a card acknowledging the fact that your suggestion has reached the proper authorities.

The Improvement Suggestion Investigators then get busy on it. They go into the whole situation very thoroughly. Every aspect is examined closely. From their action it is determined how much ingenuity was involved, how much time and money will be saved over the course of a year, and a calculation of the award is made. The final decision is reached by the Suggestion Award Committee. From their meeting comes either an award announcement certificate and a check, or a letter thanking you for your interest but pointing out that at that time they don't feel that the idea merits an award.

PLAQUE FOR HOUSEKEEPING is awarded temporarily to P Area by Fred Endorf, second from right, Reactor Department superintendent, and is accepted by J. B. Southerland, senior operator in Power. At left, Ken Leifermann, area supervisor, Power; right, Ivan Smith, P Area superintendent, Production. Power Department in P was credited with winning first phase of contest.

100 Areas Clear Decks In Housekeeping Contest

Paced by P Area with two consecutive wins, the Plant's 100 Areas cleared the deck last week for a show-down in its three-

test—running from Aug. 13 through Aug. 24—could overcome P's lead, he said.

Judges for the final phase are

Wage Checks Being Folded Improperly

SRP's card-type checks, first used last September, are making short work of a once costly and time-consuming operation. Only improper handling of the checks by a small percentage of employees prevents Machine Accounting's IBM machines from doing an even better job, according to Division Supervisor Bailey Harris.

When payroll checks are cashed, they are returned to the Accounting Department. The checks must then be matched with Payroll records. This used to be a tedious job until the card-type checks were introduced. Now IBMs sort the checks at something like 650 checks a minute.

Mutilated checks, however, jam the machines and stop the entire operation. Operators then have to clear the machines by hand.

Most of the difficulty can be eliminated, Bailey explains, if employees will be careful to fold checks only on the slighty scored

First Winners Announced In Plant Safety Contest

Betty Wilhoite, Textile 9B, C Shift, receives her prize from her Foreman, Frank Foster. Betty was the first draw winner in the big Plant-Home Safety Contest.

The range of day-to-day subjects on which the publication can call for employee aid or action is as broad as management's problems in running the enterprise. Their variety is suggested by the sampling of topics covered in the clippings above. Employees are requested to submit suggestions that will improve the organization's efficiency; a safety contest stimulates employees to work without injury; workers' support is requested for a campaign to improve area housekeeping. The host of tiny administrative difficulties a publication can resolve is typified by the article asking employees not to fold their pay checks, while a much more substantial note is struck by the clipping in which management urges a full vote in a forthcoming NLRB election.

REPLACING OUTDATED EQUIPMENT: New corrosion-resisting pyrex glass pipelines and special pumps being installed by Engineering Area One Construction mechanics, Andy Surman, left, and Ernest Snyder, will reduce upkeep costs on equipment it replaces near the Benzidine Building. Thousands of work orders involving millions of dollars were put through last year to insure that our production units would keep working at top efficiency, thus keeping final costs of our products as low as possible.

NEW AND IMPROVED METHODS: Never-ceasing search yields better ways to do our various jobs. Here is one example—a tele-typewriter which transmits sales, purchase and inventory data by wire from our Shipping Office to Wilmington headquarters and warehouse centers. It enables our clerical staff to process new orders quickly, thus speeding delivery to waiting customers. Prompt service of orders is often as important as low cost and quality in winning customer reorders. Betty Stark is the operator in photo above.

HOLD THAT LINE

Keeping Up With Competition, More Urgent Than Ever

Competition, the pulse at the heart of our enterprise system, is always with us. Even in good times, it exerts the pressure needed to keep us on our toes. And when business falls off temporarily, as it has done recently, competition quickly separates the skilled and efficient producers from the also-rans.

Keeping our plant competitive is the first step in protecting plant jobs and investment. In part, keeping competitive is the responsibility of our management. It is also, in large part, the responsibility of every employee. All members of Chambers Works must be constantly alert in holding down costs, in maintaining high product quality, and in providing customers with prompt and rapid delivery of goods they order.

Some of the ways in which management plans and works to keep our plant competitive are illustrated here. In good times and in bad, obsolete equipment must be replaced and better tools and procedures must be adopted as they become available.

Equally important, as Chambers' Works employees in these pictures make clear, every person on this plant can help our product to compete every minute he is on the job. By such efforts as the careful performance of job duties and the conservation of materials, each employee does his part in keeping our products on top in the battle for sales in the dyes, refriger-

BETTER MATERIAL HANDLING: By substituting disposable "one-way" containers such as the lightweight fiber-pack drum in foreground for heavier, costlier, steel drums, management has been able to reduce shipping costs. Such saving enables us to whittle a few more cents per pound from the price of our products. One of the newest innovations here is the 4x4x6 foot fiber "Pillar-Pak" container, being checked by shipping inspector Jim Crawford, in which 1500 lbs., of "Neazone D", an accelerator, is shipped to rubber manufacturers. Fork lift trucks, conveyers and other mechanized equipment also help increase productivity and reduce "bull work"

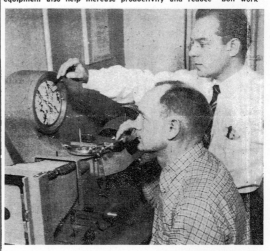

BETTER TOOLS: This new Bausch & Lomb Metallograph machine is used by the Plant Technical Section Development Lab to study structural characteristics of metal as an aid to determining causes of equipment failures and prescribing most durable compositions for new installations. Technician Ben Cates, seated, and metallurgist Bob Miller, examine greatly enlarged image, on screen, of a metal sample which is being evaluated for a specific use. The apparatus also provides for micro photographic pictures which show carbon spots, corrosion-pitting or stress and strain indications.

In the final analysis, all stories that call for employee aid in increasing organization efficiency bear upon the basic business problem of meeting competition. Any problem that management "takes to its people," obviously, is designed to help the enterprise survive in the market-place. At regular intervals, however, a good employee publication will head into the subject of competition directly, often with a roundup story of the type reprinted above. This feature, published in a time when sales were off, stressed that competition was not a problem that management could solve alone; active employee efforts were also necessary. Management's share of the dual responsibility, the editor pointed out, was to provide ever-improving methods, machines and processes; the employee in turn must do his part by following standard procedures, spotlighting quality, avoiding waste, and handling materials and tools with maximum efficiency.

Part Three

———◆———

8. Choosing the Editor

1. THE EDITOR IS THE PUBLICATION

For most companies, launching an employee publication is a venture into an unfamiliar realm, and it is not unnatural at the outset to feel some trepidation over the organization's lack of experience or special competence in this novel field.

Fortunately, the basic management principles which guide other activities effectively will also quickly set a publication on a productive course.

Prominent among these principles is the recognition that work of high quality demands top-flight personnel. Behind every well-done job, whether it be safety, scientific research, or process design, stands an uncommon individual. So it is with the employee periodical: its vigor, imagination, and depth are direct reflections of personal qualities in its editor. The impact a publication makes upon its readers will be strong or weak depending upon the talent and personal force of the man whose name is on its masthead.

It is very easy, even natural, for a busy management to overlook the importance of professional editing. One reason, of course, is that a publication is an intangible activity whose success or failure cannot be measured with mathematical precision; publication imperfections do not stand out so starkly as product flaws which a quality inspector would spot and reject on an assembly line.

Second, until recent years, most employee publications had extremely modest goals. Aiming largely to entertain or to provide readers with personal news, they did not require unusual editorial skills, but could be put together by almost any personnel man who had some time to spare.

Today, however, most managements have come to feel that publications can be economically justified only when their content is significant and when their objective is to alleviate serious plant or company problems. More and more firms are setting out consciously to interpret their operations, to instill employee pride in self and organization, and to disseminate factual information on such oft-distorted subjects as profits, investment, and productivity.

Such ambitious educational objectives broaden the dimensions of the editorial job, and search for the proper individual to do it becomes a top priority concern. For first-rate industrial editing today has become a highly creative function. The most important part of the process is mental. Applying his brain to such raw materials as company problems, management policies, or economic principles, the skilled editor selects a point, devises an approach, and presents his subject in a manner designed to attract attention and influence employee conduct. This is no simple or easily mastered routine; the product which results will always bear the unmistakable impress of the personality who created it.

Management awareness of the editor's key role is growing rapidly, of course, as indicated by the steadily rising caliber of publications personnel. A recent study by the International Council of Industrial Editors, for example, found that its typical member today is far more likely to be a "full-time" editor than his counterpart of five or 10 years ago; likewise, today's editor is found to have more education, a higher salary, and greater stature in his company than was deemed necessary only a short time ago.

This increasing emphasis upon high-grade personnel is the most important advance the employee periodical has made to date, for it focuses on the most fundamental of all facts: the higher the standards management sets for editors, the more gratifying will be the results. The editor is the publication.

2. THE MAN TO LOOK FOR

To recognize on sight the man who will become a first-class industrial editor is probably no easier than picking out the prospect who will become a brilliant process engineer. On paper, countless people may appear to qualify and few candidates will be ruled out on such grounds as personality or manner which might hamper their effectiveness in editorial jobs.

Much finer screens, therefore, are needed to choose one's editor; yet, in deciding upon editorial qualifications, the recruiter must be careful not to be too arbitrary.

For example, it is sometimes insisted that the potential industrial editor must absolutely have a "journalism background." That is, he must be a practicing newspaperman, or he must be trained in a journalism school, or he must be a good writer. This kind of preparation, it is said, insures that the candidate has mastered such tools of his trade as layout, typography, or headline writing; he will not have to learn his job at company expense,

but will be fully equipped to take over the publication on his first day of work.

This view is logical enough, but the experience of many companies indicates that technical know-how is by no means the most important thing to look for. For one thing, many individuals steeped in techniques fail as industrial editors. Second, if some of industry's best editors had been required to demonstrate technical proficiency before being employed, they would have been rejected out-of-hand. They had no formal editorial background, yet they became excellent editors.

This suggests that the man most likely to succeed is one who possesses certain basic traits of character and personal inclination. To find out what such characteristics might be, I recently undertook to analyze 30 editors pronounced "outstanding" by their managements.

What traits did those editors share in common? The first and most striking similarity they displayed was intense interest in the work they were doing. This work they conceived to be the selling of ideas; they were, in short, natural-born advocates who found constant stimulus and satisfaction in trying to increase the employee's knowledge of industry, his understanding of its history and contributions, his sympathy for its needs. Whether the story subject was a benefit plan, depreciation and obsolescence of equipment, or the problems of raising capital, it was approached with energy, enthusiasm, and the desire to excel.

The second obvious characteristic the editors shared was intellectual curiosity reflected in their broad backgrounds in such subjects as history, political science, sociology, psychology, and economics. College majors of the 30 men covered 13 different subjects, but their interests tended to spill over into several fields. Almost to a man, they were omnivorous readers, constantly looking for material and ideas which would add depth and interest to their publications. This broad liberal education turned out to be the editors' prime asset; it gave them both a fund of information upon which to draw, plus the perspective needed to interpret difficult subjects in an interesting and illuminating way.

Perhaps it was this range of interests, persisting long after college days, which gave the editors a reputation for intelligence. Certainly, I think, it lay behind the obvious fact that their publications were marked by unusual originality, freshness, and authority; their productions were never dull nor commonplace.

Finally, and perhaps most important, the 30 editors possessed that elusive quality which some managements label "judgment," and others "maturity." The editors had the capacity to inspire management confidence in their opinions and their work. And this is a vital matter. Often in the past, management has been taken to task on the grounds that it does not display enough confidence in "the editor." But it is clear that no manager can be expected to place his trust in a job title. The editor must, by his individual merits, earn respect and confidence; he cannot command them.

In sum, enthusiasm for the work, broad educational background, imagination, and personal judgment—these are the characteristics of the editor most likely to bring a high return on management's investment in publications. Such traits should always take precedence over technical training. The mechanical details of editing can be mastered well enough to operate in a few weeks or months at the most. But the mental and intellectual resources upon which the top-flight editor will draw are the product of a whole life's cultivation, and they cannot be fabricated overnight.

3. WHERE TO FIND THE EDITOR

Because management will be seeking brain power rather than purely formal skills, there is no single, treasured source of high-caliber industrial editors. As might be expected, a large number of recruits for industrial publications or other public relations activities comes from daily or weekly newspapers, magazines, and other forms of commercial journalism.

But the press is by no means the only source. When the backgrounds of the 30 editors referred to above are analyzed, only one third entered industry directly from a journalism field. The last prior employment of another third was college attendance at either the graduate or undergraduate level, while the final third had worked in fields which included politics, college publicity, teaching, radio, and sales promotion.

Former occupations of the top 10 editors among the 30, for example, were as follows: One was a graduate student in business; one a journalism student; two were college publicity men; two were newspapermen; one a congressman's assistant; one a radio announcer and writer; one a promotional secretary for a fraternal society; and one had been in the sales department of a life insurance firm.

What does this absence of an arbitrary occupational or educational pattern indicate to the recruiter? First, I think, it means he will have to look for an individual, one who combines mental power with a strong interest in selling ideas and winning support for business institutions. Second, it means that he can never be sure where the quarry will turn up: the potential editor may be in a business school, on a daily newspaper, in an advertising department, or on a college faculty.

Talent, however, is vital, and, whatever it costs, it will be the cheapest commodity management will buy. For a strong man at the helm is the only insurance that an employee publication will realize its potential as a channel of organizational communications.

4. PERSONNEL NEEDS VARY ONLY IN QUANTITY

The personnel needs of small- and large-circulation periodicals will vary principally in numbers of people, not in quality of individuals. The abilities of the plant editor, for example, should be comparable to those possessed by the staff of a company-wide publication, for management expects him to do the same kind of job. Any differences which exist will generally be in the realm of experience or seasoning as may be seen in the so-called "farm system" training adopted by Du Pont. The practice has been to assign younger men high on potential and short on experience to plant periodicals. Then larger, company-wide publications are usually staffed with the most successful editors from plants.

The actual number of people a management needs to produce a publication depends, basically, upon such varied factors as frequency of issue, format, and company geography.

For example, experience shows that a well-edited, four-page newspaper coming out biweekly needs an editor, a capable secretary, and first call on the organization photographer. A weekly newspaper, appearing twice as often, will need at least one more capable editor to handle the doubled work load.

When a management produces a periodical in magazine format, however, staff needs will be greater, for such a publication requires more painstaking preparation than a newspaper. Even though it may be a monthly, it will need at least as much talented manpower as a biweekly in newspaper format.

How a factor like company geography sometimes determines a staff's size is most clearly seen in the case of large, company-wide publications. Large staffs are essential not only because the periodical is shooting for high professional standards, but also because editors frequently travel thousands of miles per year, producing features and pictures on widely scattered plants and locations. Such a process naturally takes time and absorbs manpower.

However individual publication needs vary, one principle applies: management should take the same care in screening the second, third, or fourth editors as it did in employing the first. No periodical profits by the mere addition of persons, but only by an increase of creative effort.

Sometimes, of course, a publication attempts to keep staff needs at minimum levels by enlisting the aid of amateur reporters; about half of all house organs utilize such volunteers. But the number is declining, for, in practice, most companies find that such a system works poorly, if at all. First, the flow of material from "plant sources" or from "area reporters" is unpredictable and leaves too much to chance. Second, such material as is obtained from reporters is of low quality and generally deals with trivial matters.

This is an inevitable, though painful, outcome. The result is that, as the production of industrial publications has become professionalized, organizational reporters are either abolished or ignored. For when management's objectives for its publication become deeper and more ambitious, no aspect of production can be left to chance or to nonprofessionals.

5. HOW TO HELP THE EDITOR

What can management do to help a talented editor produce the best possible product for the organization? In addition to guidance on policy, a topic discussed in detail in the next chapter, most managements will find three practices useful in keeping the editor performing at peak efficiency:

1. **Express a continuous interest in the publication's objectives and in the editor's plans for achieving them.** Because he is a specialist, even the best editor may sometimes get the feeling that he is working alone or that his efforts are going unnoticed. A top management gesture of interest in the publication may be as invigorating to the editor as a raise in salary.

2. **Applaud inventiveness and originality; encourage the editor to keep in mind that one of his first functions is to think and plan so that each issue is fresher and more substantial than the last.**

3. **Urge the editor to take advantage of every opportunity to improve his competence and professional skills.** He should have access to publications literature, to personnel or psychological journals, and to general business magazines and newsletters. He can usually profit also by joining an association of industrial editors, particularly those which frequently sponsor useful programs, import experts to discuss new techniques and trends in the field, or perform other practical services to members.

It will quickly be seen that such modest personnel practices as these are really only stimuli to editorial achievement. And that is really all they can be. Management desire for a strong publication, however intense, can never produce one singlehanded; in the final analysis, the periodical's quality depends upon the quality of the editor in charge.

9. Determining the Publication's Content

1. CODIFYING OBJECTIVES

The first and basic requirement for an effective employee periodical is a clear-cut answer to the question, "What do we want this publication to do?"

The more concrete and realistic the reply to this question, the less likely a publication is to flounder or lose its sense of direction. The editorial course will be clear, and management hopes for a good return on the publication will be realized.

The soundest beginning, therefore, is to codify objectives—to write them down in the form of a master plan which the busy editor can repeatedly refer to in the course of his work. Such a plan may vary in its details from one company to another, but a good one should contain two principal elements: the first is a clear statement of each *major publication objective*. The second element is a concise listing of *story themes*, or policy points which publication articles should make to achieve each of the objectives.

Because a master plan is the backbone of an effective publication, devising one is a first order of business for every editor. A model which has worked well and which can be readily adapted to any management's situation is shown below. Note that the illustrated portfolio, Part II of this book, is the translation of this plan into print.

The master plan (pp. 94–95) is a pattern which any kind of organization can quickly tailor to its individual needs. Naturally, many companies will want to add story themes especially pertinent to their operations, or to make other changes. However such details may vary, every publication must be guided by a chart which tells at a glance what subjects it should be discussing and what points it should be making.

2. THE IMPORTANCE OF PLANNING

The second essential requirement for a solid and useful periodical is detailed planning to insure that the master plan is translated into stories and features. This, too, is hard mental work requiring disciplined thought against which the best mind is tempted to rebel. But there is no substitute. Every issue of a successful periodical must be as carefully and thoroughly planned as a production schedule. At every step of the process, the editor will know exactly what he is doing. When the final product appears, the reader may be struck by its air of spontaneity and freshness, but the editor and the management know that every word and every picture began life as an abstract story theme in the master plan. The point to be made determined the story to be told.

Because detailed planning, like the hidden portions of an iceberg, is not always evident at a glance, it is easy to overlook its fundamental nature. But only a publication which consciously adheres to codified objectives, issue after issue and year after year, is likely to become a serious force in a management communications program.

3. USING A PUBLICATION TO "ANTICIPATE"

A large part of any publication's content, obviously, will deal with topics which are timely and immediate. But planning, by definition, means "looking ahead," and increasingly, as industrial publications develop, their focus is upon anticipating possible future problems, misunderstandings, or disagreements. That is, editorial and management planning sessions ask questions such as these: "What can we say in the publication which will help us six months from now—or a year from now? What might become a problem? What kind of information can we provide today which will give our people a yardstick to measure future events? How can we prepare them for possible changes?"

For example, a plant whose management foresaw extensive process modernization which would affect employees began two years in advance to prepare its people for the events to come. Repeatedly, the publication reported the plant's keen competition, described the problems of product quality faced by an aging plant, and pointed to the need for an improved process. Thus, when the modernization program actually began, management encountered no employee fear, dismay, or resistance.

Similarly, a company serving a market which fluctuates suddenly and unpredictably from peak production to recession works steadily to make this fact of business life known to, and appreciated by, its employees. Another organization, anticipating possible discord on seniority at union contract time, began 12 months ahead to provide employees with some background, feeling that such information might make no

headway if it were not presented until seniority became a subject of emotional debate.

The practice of looking ahead is likewise basic to any program seeking to build employee knowledge of economic subjects affecting business. A publication's planners systematically interpret the philosophy, operations, and needs of business not merely when faced by clear and present dangers, but at all times. The object is to provide the employee with the raw materials of informed and enlightened opinion—to build a store of basic knowledge which will enable the employee to judge possible future events or evaluate the impact of legislative proposals which management might think destructive to business enterprise.

This anticipatory function of a worthwhile periodical is best likened to preventive maintenance; the goal is to prevent breakdowns rather than to repair them. There are no management problems or potential problems which the employee publication cannot help to alleviate if planned in this thoughtful and forward-looking way.

In a sense, perhaps the best management advice on planning a publication was provided more than four hundred years ago by the Italian, Machiavelli, who wrote: "When one descries afar off the evils that are brewing, they are easily cured. But when they are allowed to grow so that everyone can recognize them, there is no longer any remedy to be found."

4. THREE RULES TO KEEP A PUBLICATION ON COURSE

Even the best-intentioned publication will at times go astray and its content become diluted. One reason is the fact that an editor pressed by onrushing deadlines may begin to

MASTER PLAN

This publication will seek to achieve the four major objectives shown below. Under each of the objectives are listed the themes and policy points which the publication's features and stories should make.

OBJECTIVE NO. 1

To build the individual's pride in, and identification with, this organization.

To reach this objective, stories and features should stress the following themes:

(a) Plant products provide a valuable and worth-while contribution to the nation's people; they find a market because they are well made and supply a need;

(b) The organization's production and research achievements, records, and citations are a matter of pride for every member of the organization;

(c) The organization provides training to upgrade skills and equip employees for promotion;

(d) Management respects personal dignity and is concerned with the individual's welfare;

(e) Employee benefit plans are liberal;

(f) The organization makes every effort to provide good working conditions;

(g) Employee's years with organization have been pleasant, well spent, and productive;

(h) The organization's people do well, live well, are solid citizens;

(i) Employees enjoy a high degree of job security;

(j) The plant is a good force in the community, exerts a benign economic impact.

OBJECTIVE NO. 2

To build understanding of the nature, problems, and needs of the organization.

The publication should stress the following themes:

(a) The organization's size is determined by its function;
(b) Large and small businesses are interdependent;
(c) Huge investments in research and production facilities make possible huge contribution to nation, benefiting all;
(d) Constantly improving technology is the key to plenty;
(e) Profits provide jobs and job security;
(f) Oppressive taxation can kill incentive and limit growth.

OBJECTIVE NO. 3

To increase understanding of the role and function of the individual within the organization.

Stories should stress the following basic themes:

(a) An organization is an assemblage of individuals; it has no existence apart from people;
(b) An organization's performance is the sum of the performances of its individual members;
(c) The modern employee possesses a high degree of skill and special knowledge;
(d) The modern employee is responsible for successful operation of complex equipment and processes unheard of only a few years ago;
(e) Membership in an organization makes possible feats impossible to the individual working alone.

OBJECTIVE NO. 4

To build participation in those activities which improve the organization's efficiency and effectiveness.

Stories and features should stress the following themes:

(a) Cost-reduction keeps product prices down, markets expanding;
(b) Conservation of materials and supplies is a first step in meeting competition;
(c) Quality workmanship is foundation of job security;
(d) Safe work, good housekeeping, regular attendance, etc., build an effective team;
(e) Suggestions for improving efficiency keep plant up-to-date and progressive.

fill some of his space with material not up to proper standards. Second, employee publications usually receive much unsolicited and superficial advice from vocal individuals, and it is easy to be swayed. Likewise, there are requests for space from people or agencies one finds it hard to refuse, and finally, there is the natural human instinct to turn away from the unpleasant or the controversial.

All such temptations must be resisted if a publication is to render maximum service to management. It is, therefore, a good idea to insure that content of every issue conforms to three arbitrary rules:

1. Every article and feature should be planned to achieve the objectives the publication has set up for itself. Irrelevant or pointless material should be ruthlessly pruned as being a waste of the publication's money.

That a subject is merely "interesting" can never qualify it for admission to print; the key requirement is pertinence to the concerns of the organization. Thus, everything which goes into a periodical should be faced with the question: "How will this enhance the well-being of this plant or company?" If the editor cannot give a clear-cut answer, he must delete the item.

2. The publication's content should appeal to the broadest possible audience. Material that is significant and pertinent only to a small group or to an individual should be suspect.

Such a rule quickly helps to resolve such perennial dilemmas as whether or not to run personals, or the unsolicited, routine snapshots of deer slain by readers. With rare exceptions, such material interests only a tiny fraction of the total audience; in addition, it does nothing to interpret or improve understanding of the organization. It should, therefore, be excised.

A good editorial rule of thumb is to try to make every item as important and appealing to the office worker as it is to the shift operator.

3. A publication's content should be distinguished for complete and full coverage of plant and company matters important to readers. If it is to retain employee respect, it can never duck unhappy or controversial subject matter; content should be checked for "significant omissions" which employees will quickly detect.

It is natural and tempting to avoid discussion of the unpleasant: a layoff, for example, or pollution problems. But to ignore a topic obvious and significant to all undermines a periodical by casting grave doubts upon its honesty and credibility. In all such cases, the best policy is to present the facts, simply and straightforwardly; to put the facts into perspective; and to seek thereby to neutralize rumors and speculation. Such an approach is not only useful to the organization, but just as important, it preserves the publication's most valuable possession: its reputation for truthfulness.

10. Locating the Publication in the Organization

1. FINDING THE EDITOR'S PLACE

The editor's prime need is information. To apply his talents most effectively, he must possess a working knowledge of his institution's policies, plans, and problems. And this demands that the publication be located in the organization so that the editor has access to top-management thinking.

Because it is so easy to overlook this point, a management must take care to avoid two ever-present pitfalls: (1) setting up a periodical as an activity with ill-defined organization ties, and (2) stationing a publication at the bottom echelons of personnel or industrial relations sections.

In both cases, the editor would be hampered because the channels to top management are so long or involved that the publication is among the last to be informed of significant developments. More than that, the editor would lack the all-important guidance provided by a firsthand knowledge of management's beliefs, opinions, and general outlook.

This is not to say that a skilled and perceptive editor requires spoon-feeding or special handling to do a workmanlike job. He doesn't. But an improper location seriously complicates his tasks of acquiring vital information and adequately interpreting top leadership's point of view.

For example, one common problem of the editor located too far down in the organization is that he may have a supervisor for whom guiding the publication is an unfamiliar task foreign to his training and field of special competence. Naturally, such a man is often timid about innovations in subject matter and technique, or unduly cautious about his personal responsibility for the printed word. Often too, he finds himself in the position of making decisions on policy matters about which he has little information. Should the publication focus on plant competition? What, indeed, should it say about the pollution problem? The supervisor may not know. If he doesn't, the editor's creative talents can easily be neutralized.

A second problem created by the improper location of the editor is more subtle, but equally real: low prestige in the organization. By the place it assigns the publication, management indicates how much importance it attaches to the activity. This is inevitable. The busy works engineer, the process chief, even the shift supervisor, will take their cues from management as to how much time and priority can be devoted to publication requests. First things come first.

Low status does not necessarily hamstring the good editor, but it does make him heavily dependent upon other people's decisions. If his job's prestige is uncertain, his best-laid plans may be sent awry by a single individual's whim or lack of interest.

Because of such factors, most managements conclude that conscious action is required to keep the editor posted and to give the publication stature. Accordingly, they take the first and most important step: the publication is located so that the editor reports to one of the organization's policy makers. In an industrial plant, this individual may be the personnel superintendent or some other member of the manager's personal staff; in a company's headquarters, he may be the director of public or industrial relations activities. In either case, such a person is equipped to give the publication a sound organizational foundation, and also to provide the editor with the insight required to do intelligent, long-range planning.

2. THE EDITORIAL ADVISORY COMMITTEE

A second effective way to provide the editor with the raw materials of a good publication is to appoint an Editorial Advisory Committee composed of top-ranking representatives from each major department of the organization: production, technical, personnel, service, or sales. By virtue of their special knowledge, such men can comment intelligently on features and plans proposed by the editor; they can provide him with briefing and background, suggest points which need extra emphasis, and acquaint him with all problems which might be treated directly or indirectly in the publication.

That such committees have proved their value is indicated by a recent survey of 25 major industrial publications: 18 editors cited an advisory committee as one of their primary aids.

If such a group is to be truly effective, however, three requirements must be met. First and most important, its members must be men of substantial rank in the organization. At times, a management is tempted to name one or more committee members from people of lesser standing: from foremen in a plant or clerks in an office. But this is seldom advisable, for committeemen can be of maximum value only when they really know the institution's problems and when they have the authority required to make decisions.

The second requirement for a useful committee is that the editor assume the role of leader and adopt personal responsibility for guiding the committee's thinking into productive channels. He is the journalist and must quickly dispel a committee's natural uncertainty about what it can do to help the publication. Only silence will result if the editor provides no direction.

Many editors thus find it best to open each meeting by describing plans for the next issue, devoting special attention to major policy matters which they will cover. The editor then invites comment and suggestions.

Sometimes his committee will have little to add. Just as often, however, the member representing manufacturing will suggest a change of emphasis in the proposed article on quality, or the technical man will point out that several functions of the laboratory have been overlooked by the editor.

After all such guides and additions are recorded, the editor can pass to discussion of the pressing subjects which should be covered in the immediate future. Again, he will probably have to focus committee thinking by specific and concrete questions: "What are our primary manufacturing problems and what should we say about them? What new process developments are in the offing? What about new construction or modernization projects? What is the most important thing our people can do to meet competition?"

Finally, the editor will enlist the committee's aid in anticipating the future, as described in the last chapter: "What," he inquires, "should we be saying in the publication today which will help us six months or a year from now?" This phase of a committee meeting should never be forgotten; the conclusions reached in this discussion will be an important determinant of the long-range value of his periodical.

The third step to a smoothly working advisory committee is insuring that members understand their function as clearly as the editor understands his. The committee should conceive itself as a group of experts brought together to give the editor the benefit of its special knowledge. It should never concern itself with the details of editing—writing style, layout, typography, and allied matters; members have neither the time nor the professional training to handle the editor's job.

Just as important, the advisory committee should not assume its primary function to be the negative one of censorship. If it does, the bulk of its thinking is likely to be upon what *not* to say and this frequently means that the number of subjects which the editor can discuss steadily contracts; the simplest fact becomes cloaked in legal language and qualification, and soon the publication is largely innocuous material of no value to the organization.

Thus, it is best if management can nip all possible confusion in the bud by clearly defining the committee's function in an unequivocal way. The best technique I have seen was that of a plant manager who charged new appointees to the committee as follows: "This is a committee to use the publication. Its function is to give our people a rounded, complete view of the company and to make sure that the facts on serious subjects important to the organization's well-being are steadily presented. The committee should use the publication, and the editor should use the committee."

This is a pretty good formula.

II. Selecting the Format

1. TWO POSSIBLE CHOICES

One of the early decisions a publication-minded management must make is whether its periodical will be a magazine or newspaper. This is sometimes a subject of warm debate among editors; both types of publication have their devotees, many of whom predict semimagical benefits if their format is adopted.

Thus, the general pattern in industry is a mixed one. For the time being, the magazine has more adherents: a recent study estimates that more than 60 per cent of all house organs take this form. But it is also interesting to note signs of an increasing swing to newspapers; for example, one company which had 25 major plant magazines 10 years ago, today has only three; the rest have converted to newspaper format.

This suggests that the form an employee publication takes is determined largely by the needs and desires of the sponsoring management. Two facts are obvious and fundamental:

1. No particular format is in itself a magic formula. Magazines and newspapers alike are composed of paper, words, and pictures. The value of both will depend upon what they say to the reader rather than upon their physical appearance.

2. Employee readers do not clearly prefer one format over another. One management or employee group may swear by a magazine, while another location will insist that no magazine can match a newspaper. All this means is that people like what they are accustomed to. Those used to a magazine prefer that format, while those who have been receiving a newspaper call for more of the same. Even when management changes format, say, from magazine to newspaper, unfavorable reaction is generally short-lived. The audience quickly becomes adapted to a new routine.

To select one's format intelligently, therefore, requires that the comparative merits of magazines and newspapers be considered in detail.

2. THE MAGAZINE FORMAT

The principal reason for the popularity of the magazine is undoubtedly its handsome, substantial, and nonperishable appearance. A management naturally feels that an attractive package is a source of pride to employees; they are likely to read, preserve, and display it in their homes. Second, management senses that a magazine is desirable for its benign impact upon the company's community audience; its well-groomed appearance suggests a great deal that is favorable about the firm it represents.

These points are equally valid whether the magazine emphasizes text articles and few pictures, or whether it is a "picture story" magazine of the *Life* style in which the editor presents the bulk of his message visually through photographs.

Either type of magazine, if well done, is appealing and effective. But experience also shows that the magazine format has some very definite disadvantages as an employee publication:

1. It is expensive. When compared with the newspaper format, its costs per issue are roughly double because of the complex printing operations it requires.

2. The magazine is difficult to produce and demands more time, skill, and professional experience than an equivalent newspaper. In a picture magazine, for example, the editor is actually substituting photographs for words. This requires detailed planning, careful scheduling, painstaking layout, and compressed writing—needs felt in every publication, of course, but most acutely in a magazine.

3. A magazine's cost, plus the time required for its production, generally means that it appears less frequently than an equivalent newspaper. For example, 60 per cent of U.S. house organs are monthlies, while a sizable number are bimonthlies, or even quarterlies.

Infrequency of issue means that the magazine is of limited use to management as a channel to distribute timely information. Rarely is a magazine's production schedule flexible enough to cover sudden developments, to spearhead plant campaigns, or to provide running commentary on day-to-day topics important to the company. Rather, the magazine works best as a long-range tool whose editor is working anywhere from a month to six months ahead. Many managements thus conclude it can be most appropriately used as a company-wide publication dealing with subjects which have no immediate date line.

3. THE NEWSPAPER FORMAT

Most newspapers in business and industry are tabloids. Essentially this means that their pages are smaller* than a typical newspaper's and that they use many photographs. This format's advantages for the business firm include the following:

1. Production or "mechanical" costs are lower than the magazine's. For example, its paper is generally cheaper and its engravings of a coarser screen. More, a newspaper ties up printer's equipment for a shorter period, and many magazine operations such as binding are eliminated altogether. One plant found that, when it changed formats from magazine to newspaper, its production costs were cut from $25,000 a year to about $16,000.

2. The newspaper is relatively easy to prepare and does not require the high degree of publishing know-how demanded by the magazine format. The editor can be a younger man with less experience. Just as importantly, ease of preparation means that the newspaper is more flexible; major changes or insertions can be made at the last moment; in a pinch, the editor can cover events which occurred as late as the evening before publication.

3. The newspaper's lower cost and greater ease of production enable it to come out more frequently than a magazine. A typical industrial tabloid will appear twice a month: 24 issues a year rather than 12, or two contacts with employees for the price of one magazine. Such frequency enables the newspaper (a) to cover topical subjects effectively, and (b) to repeat its policy themes often enough to impress them deeply upon the reader.

From these comparisons, it seems clear that a management should seek primarily to

---

* Dimensions are generally about 12 by 17 inches, with 5 columns of print instead of 8. Average number of pages is 8, with range of from 4 to 16.

choose a format best adapted to its own situation, location, and problems. If frequency and timeliness are of the essence, as they will be in most plants and smaller organizations, the newspaper is the more desirable format. Where a more leisurely tempo is satisfactory and where the educational goal is predominantly long range, a magazine will often serve management's purposes better.

4. EMULATING THE BEST PUBLICATIONS

Once the publication's format is decided, the editor's prime concern becomes that of using it to maximum advantage.

Without any doubt, the best way to begin is consciously to emulate the best commercial publications in the same format. This practice sounds obvious and natural, but it is frequently overlooked, and the excellent models provided by highly successful mass circulation periodicals are ignored.

One reason, undoubtedly, is that the industrial editor senses that his purposes are different. That is true; essentially he is trying to inform or persuade his readers, while commercial periodicals are seeking primarily to entertain. But format is a mechanical matter, a question of physical appearance. Without vitiating his content in the slightest, the industrial editor can adopt the commercial publication's masterful techniques of presentation.

Perhaps the basic physical characteristic an industrial editor will imitate is layout—the way in which a commercial publication arranges its stories and pictures into an arresting and appealing display. To insure that this job is done well, mass-circulation magazines employ art directors and daily newspapers appoint make-up editors. These specialists the typical industrial publication cannot afford,

but it can benefit by their skills at all times by paying close attention to their work in first-rate periodicals. For example, the editor of an industrial picture magazine should always study *Life* and *Look* carefully. A text-and-picture-magazine editor can profitably examine the layouts of *The Saturday Evening Post* or *The Ladies Home Journal;* while the editor of a tabloid newspaper can ponder the *New York Daily News.**

If the editor combines what he observes of the best professional practices with the advice and experience of a good printer, his format is not likely to suffer from inept layout—particularly if he always follows three basic rules:

1. Whatever his format, the industrial editor should never permit the layout of his pages to become a matter decided by chance. To do so naturally invites slapdash presentation of his content. In the press of production, of course, it is easy to postpone thoughts of layout until type is set and engravings are made. But such last-minute efforts seldom produce satisfying results: there are too many cuts for one page, or headlines are set in too large a type face, or the page is top-heavy and unattractive. Such problems are easily avoided if page designs are planned before the raw materials are actually purchased.

2. Always provide oneself and the printer with layout sheets or a "dummy" perfect to the last detail. With such a tool, the editor can write his text, headlines, and captions to fit a predetermined space, and he will not have to cut and fill later. Likewise, the printer cannot possibly go astray and expensive alter-

---

* The tabloid editor should also study magazines, for most tabloids for employees are hybrids, having the shape of a half-size daily, the paper stock of a magazine, and a layout technique which incorporates features of both.

ations, resetting of type, and juggling of engravings are unnecessary.

3. Whatever one's format, layout should be simple, direct, and as uncomplicated as possible. An editor, being human, sometimes feels that if a layout is tricky with fancy borders, montage photographs, or odd-shaped engravings, he has a good page. But he probably hasn't. The object of layout should always be to assist the reader to read; he should have no difficulty determining which headline and picture goes with which story, or which feature is most important. The editor indicates such things by the way in which he puts his materials together—that is, the way in which he lays out his page.

In layout, as in every other aspect of employee publications, the best guarantee of success is straightforward treatment of top-quality materials.

12. Setting Up the Production Budget

1. THE SEQUENCE OF DECISIONS

The process of setting up the production budget for a publication is best broken down into three steps. The first is to define clearly the job one wishes a publication to do for the organization. The second is to decide what format, frequency, and publishing schedule are most likely to achieve the objectives set. And the third step is to submit one's specifications to several reputable printers to find out what such a product will cost.

The sum arrived at after competitive bids will be the publication's production budget.

That costs are last in this sequence does not mean that, to sponsor a publication, a management must become spendthrift. Rather, it means that a publication should be installed only after a management has decided that it needs one's help and when it faces problems which it thinks a publication can help to alleviate. Costs—which in no case will be extraordinary—should not assume undue weight in the decision to publish. One spends what is necessary.

Thus, if a company, in reviewing printers' bids, is reluctant to spend the sums required to do the job it envisioned, it is usually wiser to postpone publication than to pare its objectives drastically. No periodical at all is better than one whose ambitions are not adequate to the need; and, although high cost is no guarantee of quality, a budget trimmed too low will, in most cases, defeat the purpose.

Hard-and-fast figures on printing and en-graving charges are, of course, impossible to cite because such costs vary considerably with geographical location. The rule of thumb is that costs are higher in or near large cities, higher in the West than the East, and lower in the South than the North. Within a given area, the so-called "mechanical" costs will be roughly competitive. The differences between bids of one firm and another will reflect the quality of work each intends to do, the care with which the periodical will be processed, and the service the printer provides his customers.

There are exceptions, of course. Sometimes bids will vary sharply within a given area because of the business situation or the motives of an individual printer. For example, the size of one printer's presses and equipment may be better suited to a small job than a large, and this may mean lower costs for an employee publication. Not infrequently, a printer will shave his charges to the bone with the idea that he may thereby attract other business from the company concerned; or he may seek to profit by the prestige of producing a handsome publication; or finally, he may wish to attract other and more profitable house-organ business by making a showpiece of his first project.

But even if a company is to be the beneficiary of some such unusual bounty, it is always advisable, before awarding contracts, to look beyond the actual dollar figure and focus on the kind of service being offered.

2. CHOOSING A PRINTER

Experience shows that an employee publication should be contracted only to a reputable firm which has the equipment, the time, and the desire to do a good job. With rare exceptions, a periodical should never be awarded to a printer who plans to sandwich it between "big jobs," or to fit it in when the machines are idle. The reason is obvious: for a good-sized printing firm, a single employee publication does not necessarily represent a major account—perhaps $12,000 to $20,000 a year. When this is the case, it will usually run second in the printer's affections to a larger account; lacking the attention and care it should have, the employee periodical will seldom be produced on schedule or without blemishes. It is a convenience for the printer, but a source of unending frustration to management.

A second reason for choosing a printer who is anxious to do one's company publication is that he can be of great assistance to the editor. The printer is an expert on the commodity which management is buying; he has met and solved most printing problems hundreds of times; he can and will take over the entire burden of production. Sometimes, of course, management and editor alike may vaguely feel that the editor should be a printing authority. He can't be and needn't be. He should have an accurate idea of the steps by which his periodical is produced, but he should never have to spend a disproportionate amount of time pushing through the actual printing of his paper.

Many well-trained editors report that, on a routine issue, they may see the printer only twice: once on the scheduled day when they take copy to him, and again when they return corrected and approved proof sheets for final printing. It should never be necessary for the editor to spend a day hanging around the print shop.

3. FOUR WAYS TO CONTROL COSTS

Once a budget figure is decided upon, it naturally becomes important to control the publication so that it stays within its financial bounds. This is largely a matter of orderly and systematic editorial practices, four of which are common and basic:

1. Make certain that all parties concerned with production know how much money is to be spent. Most editors find that a good procedure is to apportion the total budget over a year's issues, arriving at a per-issue figure of which the printer and the engraver are fully apprised. With such a guide, the printer can warn the editor in advance if his plans for a particular issue appear likely to run over the agreed-upon figure; or, if a special issue absorbs more than its quota of dollars, the printer can help the editor decide how to make up the difference by minor economies in future issues.

2. Make certain that the printer and the engraver know exactly what the editor wants them to do. When the editor delivers publication copy, his text and captions should be written to fit a space he has designated, thus avoiding expensive author's alterations; his photographs should be marked for cropping and be properly labeled for the engraver. Finally, the editor should provide the printer with detailed layout sheets showing where each story element of the publication should go. If there is no guesswork required, the printer cannot go wrong and costly rejects and reruns will not be necessary.

3. Keep in mind that time is really money, both for the printer setting type and preparing forms for the press and for the engraver translating photos and drawings into plates. This means that the editor should try to simplify graphic arts work by keeping it as "mechanical" as possible. For example, most type is set by machine. Unless he is careful, the editor can spend large sums merely by specifying type faces which must be set by hand and consequently take much longer to compose.

Similarly, an engraver's charges are usually based upon fixed scales for routine, "square-finish" engravings. Each time he must put his artist to work strengthening weak photos, or making intricate cuts, or doing other kinds of time-consuming engraving chores, costs mount rapidly—literally by the minute.

4. Avoid the use of "showy" or ultra-expensive printing and engraving. Most employee publications are comparatively "short runs" of 10,000 copies or less; per issue costs are accordingly high. Extra charges for special printing and engraving which would be negligible if apportioned over a run of, say, 50,000, assume mammoth proportions in a small-circulation publication. They should thus be used sparingly, else they will eat up the bulk of the budget.

A case in point is the printing of color photographs. Color is, without question, attractive, appealing, and an excellent device for giving emphasis to an article. But color in a photo requires expensive process engravings and usually four runs through the press; color reproduction will cost five or six times more than the same photograph in black and white. The typical publication simply will not be able to make such an outlay and keep its costs under control.

Naturally, the same fact applies to other specialized techniques which require unusual effort, labor, or press time. Most employee periodicals, therefore, will want to put their trust not in elaborate aids from the graphic arts industry, but in substantial content simply presented.

In the light of these conclusions, it becomes clear that, once a publication is launched, the two requisites for efficient production are an editor and a printer who know their businesses. They are equipped to make realistic and economical decisions on the proper mode of printing, the quality of paper stock required, the relative fineness of screen needed for engravings, and all other related matters of production.

But no publication's sponsor can ever lose sight of the fact that the most important financial decision of all is the original one made by management: to earmark enough money at the outset to enable a publication to capture attention, meet its competition for employee attention, and do the job it sets out to do.

13. Creating the Point-Making Feature

1. THE SHORTAGE OF NEWS

Among industrial editors, there is an oft-told tale of the man who had still not produced a newspaper six weeks after he had been employed. When his boss inquired why, he replied, "Well, basically, I'm waiting for something to happen."

This tale amuses editors because they know that an adequate supply of natural-born news events is rarely found in industry. "News" is a dramatic or startling interruption of the ordinary course of events, a notable departure from the routine. In industry, apart from negative items such as strikes, the nearest approximation to "big news" would be a plant expansion, a major organization change, or a donation to a hospital fund. Such things do not happen every day, and certainly not often enough to fill up a paper.

The result is that the bulk of the "ready-made" news which comes unbidden to the editor will usually be of a minor nature. That is, employees will reach service anniversaries, they will retire, and they will be promoted; a shift will set a safety or quality record, and the company baseball team will win the pennant. All such things are news, have some significance, and should be reported in the publication. But seldom will such events, occurring on a hit-or-miss basis, contribute substantially to the major objectives the publication has set for itself.

Where his major features and policy subjects are concerned, therefore, the industrial editor will almost always have to create his own news—to set up events conceived to make a desired point, register a favorable impression, or demonstrate an important policy proposition.

This necessity is not always obvious to industrial people. Because a first-rate employee newspaper bears a close physical resemblance to its commercial counterparts, it is often believed to operate in an identical manner—that is, it reports "what happens." But this is untrue because an employee publication's purposes are entirely different from those of a commercial periodical.

A daily, commercial newspaper, for example, sells a commodity called "news." It describes what is happening in the town, the state, the nation, and the world. It also sells entertainment: comic strips, crossword puzzles, features about celebrities, and rare or unusual persons, places, and events. The better it supplies the demand for such commodities, the more readers it attracts; its circulation rises and its advertising revenue increases.

The large-circulation commercial magazine is even more closely focused upon supplying a commodity the reader desires. All the resources of editorial intuition and genius, market surveys and psychological studies are directed to finding out more accurately what people will buy. In an ideal state, a magazine's editors would know exactly what their readers wanted, and they would then unfailingly supply it.

The industrial house organ, however, sets out to do an entirely different kind of job. Its function is not to entertain or to provide news *per se*, but to educate—to spread information and win acceptance for ideas which will enhance the welfare of the company which supports it. Its articles, of course, will have the form and flavor of news, for that will give the publication freshness and reader appeal. But its "news" will be primarily a device—a vehicle for carrying ideas—and such news will have to be created.

2. CREATING NEWS

To create news with a point, the house-organ editor begins with a clear knowledge of his purposes and the points he wants to register with readers. Then he sets out to find ways to dramatize them. One editor describes the process thus: "I create a situation, and then I report it."

To set up a situation from which a significant, newsworthy feature can be developed, most editors of experience will adopt conscious and standard techniques of which management should be aware. Following are four which add zest to an important, but apparently newsless, subject:

1. Causing something to happen, or getting people to do something which can be reported. This is the single most important tool in the editor's kit and takes many forms, as illustrated by the hypothetical story openings below. In each case, the point of the story is italicized.

"The Fred Smith family visited a string of downtown stores last week to see at firsthand *the keen competition our product faces for consumer dollars.*"

"Tim Jones, first employee hired in this plant's construction days, toured the new Area B site yesterday to see *what changes are contemplated in our process.*"

"Young Jimmy Matthews (son of me-chanic Bill Matthews) who is contemplating a science career visited our process men the other day to find out at firsthand *the facts about the shortage of technically trained people.*"

In all such stories, the tourists' findings and adventures were initiated by the editor who then reported them in pictures and text.

This technique can be adapted equally well to shorter features. For example, a caption under an impressive photo of plant supplies might read, "The mammoth heap of materials delivered to Stores Clerk Al Jones in 60 minutes yesterday *gives an idea of how large a customer this plant is for local businessmen.*"

2. Quote eminent persons or plant experts. The opinions of authorities or experts are always interesting; i.e., newsworthy, however commonplace the actual sentiments may be. If Joe Di Maggio or Senator Smith or Company President William Barnes makes a statement, it is news. This means that the editor will frequently describe problems or interpret policy by quoting company authorities. For example, "Mounting competition in our markets demands top-flight workmanship from every person in our business," Plant Manager Al Peterson told the *News* in an interview today.

3. The use of impressive numbers or statistics. To draw attention to the merits of a company savings plan, for example, the editor may do a feature "announcing" that Jack Jones is the one-hundredth person to receive a share of stock under the plan. Or, to remind readers of the merits of the broad company health program, he may describe the adventures of the ten-thousandth employee to receive a physical examination. Likewise, to create awareness of the important job done by the Power Department, the editor may announce that "the six-billionth kilowatt of electricity was pumped into the plant yesterday."

Almost always, such statistics come to light as a result of editorial digging, of course.

4. The use of surveys, straw votes, analyses, or special studies. This is one of the easiest and most interesting ways to get a story started. It can be used to make a point on practically any subject and involves merely polling a cross section of people, or citing the findings of a management study. For example: "Quality consciousness is the most welcome trait in a fellow employee, a *News* survey of company people reveals." Or, "Finger injuries are the plant's prime safety problem, a new analysis by the Central Safety Committee shows." Or, "Plant people are using up gloves at the shocking rate of six pairs per employee per year, a study by the Cost-Reduction Committee reveals."

In each case, the editor can then go on to discuss in detail the rest of the newsworthy study which, in most cases, he initiated himself.

3. THE QUEST FOR IDEAS

From the preceding, it will be apparent that the policy portions of a strong employee publication are "devised." Events which demonstrate an important point or contribute to understanding seldom happen of themselves and the publication which leaves the initiative to fortune will find itself providing its readers with pretty thin fare.

This places a premium upon constant effort to utilize the techniques cited above, and also to devise other fresh ways to introduce the themes which he must endlessly repeat in major stories. The editor, therefore, conducts a perennial quest for ideas, for what is known

in the trade as "gimmicks," or novel angles and points of departure for publication features.

There are two primary sources of such ideas:

1. The brain of the editor himself. Out of the mind of a talented editor will come a flood of astonishing proportions. Not long ago, I complimented an editor on a highly original story making the point that product quality is the twin of job security. He replied in humorous despair that "I have now told this story 211 times, and the barrel's bottom has been scraped clean." It wasn't, though. Six weeks later, he repeated the quality theme from another stance.

The importance to management of an editor with such imagination cannot be overemphasized, for he will be mirrored in his product.

2. The second, often overlooked, source of good ideas is other publications. The Old Testament observation that there is nothing new under the sun is a truth which the skilled industrial editor fully appreciates. Not only will he exchange publications widely with other companies and industries, but he will also systematically examine commercial publications for story angles or ideas which can be adapted to his uses. When he comes upon a story lead, a headline, an advertisement, or a witticism or a photograph which strikes him with special force, he should quickly store it in his future file. At some later date when his brain is cold and he needs a fresh approach, a dip into his files will often provide exactly what he needs.

Sometimes a manager will discover that his editor is reluctant to adapt ideas, feeling that imitation is a reflection upon his own powers of invention. This is a notion which management should discourage. Stimulating devices and techniques should be welcomed whatever their origin. The only test they should pass is the question, "How effectively or interestingly will this gimmick help me to tell the story I want to tell?"

To these two primary sources of editorial ideas, large companies often make one addition worthy of mention, and that is the "editorial advisory service."

In multi-plant organizations, their distance from headquarters makes it difficult for outlying editors to keep abreast of top management thinking on subjects of concern to the company. To remedy this problem, editorial aids of varied nature are frequently instituted. In some cases, such a service stresses up-to-the-minute news and maintains close teletype connections with plant editors. Other organizations, of which Du Pont is an example,

focus principally upon providing editors with story ideas, picture-story suggestions, and other data which have no fixed date line, but can be developed into local features over a period of several months.

In addition to supplying a flow of news and ideas, such services also usually conduct training programs, circulate reports of successful editorial practices, and provide general guidance and advice on publications production. They are thus quite useful agencies in large companies.

Smaller or more compact firms which do not face problems of communication with widely scattered locations will not require such a service. But there is no doubt that they will want in some way to perform one of its principal functions: stimulating the editor to create fresh, interesting, and newsworthy ways to register significant information.

14. Varying the Way a Story Is Told

Not long ago, an employee magazine did a striking "fashion fad" feature in which a pretty secretary repeatedly transformed her appearance by putting on a succession of wigs. Each time she altered the color and style of her hair, she looked like an entirely different person.

In many ways, it seems to me that the secretary's use of assorted wigs is like the industrial editor's use of the varied types of features, stories, and artwork available to him. His basic materials, i.e., his publication's themes, seldom change and must be repeated over and over. But to intrigue and attract the reader, the editor constantly changes his themes' appearance in print by varying the packages in which they are wrapped.

Thus, over a period of time he may stress an important point by presenting it in any or all of a wide range of editorial features. Prominent among them will be the types described below.

1. NEWS STORIES

Much of the material in an industrial publication will appear as news. The reasons: reading a newspaper is a daily habit for most Americans and, in addition, industrial readers are deeply and naturally interested in learning of all developments, changes, conditions, or improvements which affect their jobs.

Sometimes news will spring from a spontaneous event; often, it will have to be created by the editor, as described in the preceding chapter. In both cases, the industrial news feature should do more than provide the employee with surface data or "the top of the news." It also presents the facts behind the facts, interpreting the meaning and significance of the events or situations being reported.

For example, a news story announcing a new benefit plan will aim not merely to impart the superficial facts, but also to win employee approval and appreciation of the plan itself. Similarly, an article applauding a feat of quality workmanship intends not only to recognize a single group's achievement, but also to stimulate like performance in other groups.

A story that does less is probably not a very strong or useful addition to the publication.

2. THE EDITORIAL

In the "editorial," the writer sheds the traditional role of mere reporter and expresses subjective, personal opinions. He comments on events, takes a stand for one point of view or another, or urges adoption of a desired course of action.

Because it is a familiar feature which most readers expect to see, the well-done editorial can be a useful device to draw special attention to any significant topic. Its only weakness for an industrial publication is that, in unskillful hands, it easily becomes "preachy" and, by irritating or boring the reader, may do more harm than good. Here again, the impact of the feature will depend largely upon the finesse of the editor. Perhaps the best general advice on the subject came from the late H. L. Mencken who observed that there is nothing wrong with the editorial page which a good editorial won't cure.

3. MANAGEMENT INTERVIEWS

The principle that "big names make news" has earlier been cited as one the industrial editor should always keep in mind. Accordingly, an increasingly large number of periodicals find it profitable to feature repeated interviews with top managers or company experts in special fields. Presented in question-and-answer form, such an interview can discuss frankly and forthrightly a wide range of topics important to the organization. The eminence of the person whose views are reported gives weight to the sentiments expressed.

To keep an interview story unified and coherent, the editor should always carefully decide the theme of the feature in advance and establish firmly in his mind what topics he will cover. Some editors, in fact, keep themselves and the manager on the track by providing the subject with a list of interview-questions several days in advance; others draft a skeleton for the story before the interview begins, and the actual discussion then simply hangs meat on the bones.

Such mechanics, of course, will vary widely with the organization and the individual being interviewed. But the basic principle never changes: the object is to capitalize on the fact that readers are always interested in hearing what a notable person says about a significant subject.

4. MANAGERS' COLUMNS

In recent years, it has become the fashion to jest at "The President's Page" or the "Plant Manager's Column" as a repository of plati-tudes and aimless good will. That such features have been done badly does not mean that they cannot be done well. A good one can steadily impart significant information, provide insight into management's thinking, and acquaint employees with present or potential problems. When such substantial and rewarding fare is the rule, the manager's column is often the best-read feature in the paper.

Most companies find that such columns deteriorate quickly if they become routinized or appear in every issue. Thus, when the manager feels that there is no particular topic he wishes to comment upon, and when the editor has no suggestions for subject matter, there should be no attempt at a column. Usually the best policy is to run the manager's column often enough to keep it familiar, but infrequently enough to insure that employees always find it a source of important information and opinion which is "straight from the top."

5. QUESTION-AND-ANSWER FEATURES

A highly popular and useful feature in most publications is one which prints the answers to questions raised by employees on major policy subjects. Usually headed, "We've Been Asked . . ." or "What's The Answer?", this flexible device gives the editor an opportunity to illumine any topic or subject upon which management believes light should be shed.

Sometimes questions call for a brief answer; viz., "How much did the company put into the Pension Fund last year?" followed by the quick reply, "Just over $77,000,000, or five per cent more than any prior contribution." Just as easily, however, the question can raise a topic to be discussed at length;

viz., "What's the difference between depreciation and obsolescence?"

Where do such questions come from? The feature works most effectively when the editor phrases the queries himself after pondering supervisors' reports of questions they've been asked, and after talks with management indicate which topics should get top priority in the publication.

6. THE INQUIRING REPORTER

A valuable feature which is quite susceptible to damage through inept handling is the "Inquiring Reporter" or "Vox Pop" columns found in many publications. The procedure here is simple: six to 10 employees are asked to comment on a subject raised by the editor, and their photos and opinions are printed in the paper.

Clearly this device can be no better than the question which the editor poses. All too often, the employee is asked to comment on a completely innocuous subject: "Which team will win the pennant?", "Who is your favorite person?", "Why did you choose bowling as a hobby?" The most imaginative reply to such questions as these will enrich no one.

On the other hand, a publication can ask a question which is equally ludicrous because its intent is obviously self-serving: "Which of our many benefit plans do you think is the most wonderful?", and others of this stamp.

The editor's challenge is to devise a serious question which, without seeming to, demands a thoughtful and constructive reply. "What do you think the plant can do to meet competition?", or, "What would you say are the three prime requirements for a successful business?", or "What can the individual do to improve our safety performance?"

One of the primary virtues of the well-conceived employee-interview feature is that it inspires meditation among the rest of the organization's people. Most editors find that readers tend to "match opinions"; sentiments expressed by a few featured individuals stimulate the readers to stop for a minute and articulate an opinion of their own. In effect, the editor is asking every reader to decide what *he* thinks makes a successful plant or what *he* thinks the individual can do to improve the safety record.

Thus, one often sees a question along these lines: "What was your biggest day with the company?" Replies to such a query will vary widely, but it really makes no difference whether the employee decides his biggest day was the one on which he was employed, or received a promotion, or won an award. The important fact is that he stopped and consciously reviewed the positive aspects of his job and career—and so did most of the readers.

7. CARTOONS AND ARTWORK

Well-executed artwork adds variety and appeal to any publication and is always useful if carefully planned to say something worth saying. When cartoons in employee periodicals seek merely to evoke laughter, they are like joke columns proper, usually a waste of space.

But artwork need not represent dollars down the drain. The artist's pen is far more flexible than the photographer's camera, and imaginative art can serve a vast range of educational purposes. Examples of the ways it can be used are seen in the illustrated portfolio of this book.

8. FILLERS AND BOXES

"Fillers" are short one- or two-sentence capsules of information used in newspapers to complete a column where the major story does not "fill." In daily newspapers, fillers usually present an odd or entertaining fact of no particular consequence. In the industrial publication, however, the filler can register point-making information with a serious objective. A typical example might say, "The company's investment in tools and equipment is now $25,000 per employee," or, "Steady paychecks for 25 years is the boast of 800 employees in the plant Veterans' Club."

A "box," one editor says, is a filler grown tall. Its purpose is to register important information in three or four sentences, and it takes its name from the fact that it is boxed in by printer's rules. In industrial publications, the first sentence of a box will generally announce the point to be made; the remaining two or three sentences are documentation. For example, a typical box might say, "How research dollars create thousands of new jobs can be seen in our own company. Half our sales today are in products unknown 20 years ago; to produce them, employment has trebled, from 8,000 two decades ago to 24,000 today."

9. JOB PRIDE FEATURES

An important function of the employee periodical is to increase the individual's knowledge of his organization and his pride in his job. To supplement major features pursuing such goals, many editors often run a series of one-picture-and-caption stories headed, "This Is My Job," or "This Is My Responsibility."

The procedure is simple: the editor makes an attractive photo of an operator or mechanic at work on his job. Then, clearly and interestingly, he describes the man's responsibilities, his special knowledge and skills, and the role he plays in producing a quality product. The more specific and concrete the details cited, the more effective the article will be.

Individuals chosen to be featured in this way may either possess unusual skills or they may represent a job done by large numbers of people. In both cases, the purpose will be the same: to stress the dignity of the individual and the significance of the job he is doing.

10. SPECIAL PAGES OR BALANCE FEATURES

Both in newspapers and magazines, it is common practice to run special features whose principal purpose is to balance the heavier policy articles found elsewhere in the paper. For example, a plant with several thousand female employees may find that a "Woman's Page," replete with fashion photos and recipes, has great appeal, while an organization with an active recreation program will lean to a sports page or a hunting-and-fishing column.

When used thoughtfully, such material can serve a worth-while purpose in the employee publication, but, to avoid wasting space, it is important for the editor to keep three things in mind at all times:

1. To provide entertainment is not the publication's function; features which have no direct connection to primary objectives are printed *only* to attract readers into the publication's pages.

2. Wherever possible, the social or economic significance of the subjects discussed in balance features should be suggested in the copy. That is, a story describing unusual auto trips taken by employees can also appropriately note the benefits brought to the family by mass production of autos; a feature on women's fashions can observe that improved family wardrobes of today reflect high living standards; while plant sports features should always associate such activities with the recreation program sponsored by the company.

3. All balance material should have a local flavor and appeal. For example, recipes in the women's column should be obtained from employees or the wives of employees rather than from advertising boiler plate received in the mails; fashion pictures should feature employees as models; and sports coverage should be restricted to the activities of the local recreation program.

11. RUMOR PAGES

Examination of the varied features described above will indicate that the devices by which an editor achieves his goals are limited only by the editorial imagination. A technique should have to pass only the pragmatic test: that is, it works in one's own situation.

This means, naturally, that no technique or story-type should ever be adopted without adequate reflection. A dramatic or startling device that works in one setting may not do so well in another.

A case in point is that much debated feature, the "rumor and gripe" page in which disgruntled employees are encouraged to send complaints to the editor who attempts to answer them in print. Here, the fact that management surrenders control of the feature must be counted as the first disadvantage; in addition, such a practice often produces a page of abusive letters in which employees assail the intelligence of their foremen, the policies of management, or industrial life in general.

Among the reasons cited in favor of such a feature are (1) that it provides recognition for the employee's point of view, and (2) that rumors, frustrations, or gripes wither when they come face to face with printed rebuttals.

But many managements would question the efficiency of deciding by a comparatively small sampling of letters what the bulk of employees are thinking; likewise, they might think it possible that "gripes" are dignified by print and that a barrage of printed personal irritations can easily be mistaken for evidence of major management shortcomings. One war plant manager told me that, in such a feature, his own staff found more rumors and broadcast more vilification than the most hostile union newspaper.

For such reasons, most companies will probably decide that the way to handle "gripes" is in positive and private fashion through the medium of line organization. If the disgruntled employee really wants satisfaction and not personal publicity, his complaints can be answered by supervision.

The employee publication can indeed help to dispel misunderstandings revealed by rumors and complaints; but most managements find it works best when it presents information in a manner clouded by as little emotion as possible.

15. Planning Pictures that Tell a Story

1. THE POINT-MAKING PHOTO-GRAPH

One of the most striking characteristics of U.S. publications today is their generous use of pictures. This is evident not merely in *Life* and *Look*, but also in the broad range of general magazines and in the daily press. It is likewise evident in industrial publications: a recent survey of 2,000 company editors found that 64 per cent had steadily increased their use of pictures over the past few years.

The basic reason for the camera's popularity, of course, is the fact that a picture makes a powerful, direct appeal to the senses and emotions of the reader. He actually sees people and events with his own eyes, and the impression he gets thereby is likely to be far more vivid and moving than one provided by verbal description.

In addition, pictures offer especially rich rewards to the industrial editor because they deliver his message with ease and speed. The typical reader wants to get his information quickly, with a minimum of hard work. He would far rather look at a photograph than read a column of text. Words require concentration. In many topics which a good employee publication will discuss, words may actually call for hard intellectual labor. Thus, every time an editor substitutes a picture for prose, he magnifies his chances of making an impact and of meeting the keen competition he faces for employee time and attention.

A profusion of pictures, however, means little. To be admitted to the employee publication, photographs, like text, must advance the job which the editor is doing. And this means that a good industrial photo should always state a fact, convey an idea, or demonstrate a point which helps to achieve the periodical's basic objectives.

Very few pictures shot at random or on a hit-or-miss basis will satisfy such a condition, so the industrial editor must plan his photographs with the same care and precision which he devotes to the other content of his publication.

Generally, he will use pictures in one of two ways. He may print them singly or in combinations of two or three to illustrate text articles. In such features, pictures play second fiddle to words; their purpose is largely to emphasize a point which is being made verbally.

Alternatively, the editor can use photographs to construct a story in which pictures supplant text as the principal element; any words the editor writes are brief and aim merely to illuminate the photographs.

Whichever is called for, the editor must undertake detailed planning, and this always begins with deciding his story purpose. The editor asks himself such questions as these: "What point should these pictures make? What should they say to the reader? What fact, impression, or theme do I want them to register?"

With the purpose of his pictures well established in his mind, the editor's next step is to find ways to make them interesting and

116

appealing to the reader. Here, he will be concerned with such matters as insuring that the pictures have technical quality—that they are sharply focused, well lighted, and interestingly composed. He will insist that they have "human interest"—that they depict the activities and interests of people. Finally, he will plan to give his pictures "eye appeal," sparing no pains to find an unusual setting, to devise striking action, or to locate an off-beat camera angle. At all times, he seeks to enhance the visual impact of his photos and, hence, the effect of his message.

2. PLANNING THE PICTURE STORY

By far the most complicated planning job the editor will undertake is that required for the picture story. He quickly finds that no detail can be left to chance; every photograph must be conceived and executed so that it contributes to the flow of the story and to the total impression it makes.

Every editor will develop his own methods for planning such a feature, and any system that works is a good one. The best technique I have come upon was described by an experienced editor who likens production of a picture story to the production of a play. He begins by deciding clearly what his story, i.e., play, is going to say to the audience. Then he visualizes a series of scenes in which people are shown performing actions which demonstrate or document the editor's point and lead inevitably to his conclusion.

The play analogy, I think, is especially valuable because it provides an orderly and systematic way by which the editor can settle the countless details which must be covered by picture-story planning.

For example, one of the editor's first steps is "casting" or choosing actors for his feature. He should have very clear ideas about the kind of people he needs to make his point. If he wants to register the fact that industrial families enjoy a high standard of living, he will need employee models whose appearances, homes, youngsters, or hobbies make the desired impression beyond the shadow of a doubt. Likewise, if he wants to dramatize his company's mammoth investment in equipment per employee, he will not choose a clerk whose tool is a pencil, but an operator who runs a huge and visually impressive piece of equipment. Whatever the point, correct casting helps to make it.

Second, like the play producer, the editor must decide in advance how his people should be costumed for each scene in his story. Clothes proverbially make the man; certainly they are often decisive in determining the impression a picture makes. Dirty work clothes can imply poor working conditions. Tasteless or shabby garb can suggest low living standards. An overdressed secretary can imply an inefficient or frivolous office. For such reasons, the editor thinks very hard about the costumes his employee-models wear, for such details often make or break his feature, either contributing to, or distracting from, the main point he set out to register.

Third, the editor will have to decide upon "sets," or locations where pictures will be made. In a stage production, the set immediately tells the audience something about the story—where the action takes place, whether it is about a rich or poor family, whether the household is orderly or otherwise. Similarly, the settings of pictures in industrial publications give the reader a great deal of information. A clean maintenance shop or a bright, attractive cafeteria says good working conditions; a comfortable, cheerful employee home suggests high living standards. Clearly, the point of any story will be greatly strengthened or disastrously weakened by the setting in which it takes place.

Fourth, the editor must decide upon "props" or other symbols which he will add to each picture to make its meaning unmistakably clear. For example, a photo showing a man setting off on a fishing trip should prominently feature such props as rods and tackle, hipboots, bait, and perhaps a boat. A picture of a pipe fitter will include such story-telling symbols as a huge wrench and a background which is a maze of pipes.

In addition, of course, a principal function of good props is to magnify the reader's impression of a setting. For example, if the editor is demonstrating employee well-being by photographing an attractive home, the impression is heightened if the family's new car is parked in the driveway. No time spent upon introducing such point-making props into a picture is lost time, for such elements can add substantially to the photograph's effect.

Finally, the editor must decide in advance upon the "action"—upon what his people will be doing in the pictures. This will always be determined by the point to be made. If the editor's object is to show people having fun, the picture should show them gleefully running into the surf, or singing lustily around the piano at home, or obviously enjoying themselves dining out; certainly his people will not look glum or lethargic. Likewise, to document an employee's cultural interests, a picture should show him visiting an art gallery or buying tickets to a concert. To convey that a company medical program guards employee health, the photo subject should be shown getting a chest X-ray or physical examination.

Action, like casting, costuming, setting, and props, must always be designed to register the editor's predetermined point.

Concrete and specific decisions on all such matters should be arrived at long before picture-taking begins. Then, when the editor dispatches the photographer, he can be confident that his feature will achieve the desired objective, for his planning has left nothing to chance. All is provided for, including possible lapses of memory, for he will have wound up by preparing a "shooting script." Such a script records the point of each photo and gives a detailed description of its content; the photographer understands exactly what he is to bring back and is, therefore, free to concentrate his energies on turning out a product which is technically and artistically good.

3. OBTAINING GOOD PHOTOGRAPHY

From the foregoing, it is apparent that an absolute requirement for an effective publication is a source of good photographs. If it lacks the services of a qualified photographer, a periodical will labor under a well-nigh insuperable handicap. No matter how well and thoroughly the editor plans, his picture stories will go awry because his thinking is ineptly translated into photographic prints.

Accordingly, publications undertake to satisfy their demand for quality in one of three principal ways:

1. Hire an outside cameraman from a local studio. If the photographer chosen is skilled and imaginative, this practice often works fairly well. However, it is usually expensive and frequently complicates the editor's scheduling problems because the photographer has other clients to satisfy. In addition to planning his own and the featured employee's time, the editor must arrange his timetable to suit the photographer. For the publication on a tight schedule, this easily becomes a frustrating and impossible situation.

2. Editor attempts to double in brass as a cameraman. This solution to the photography problem is frequently adopted by smaller publications and sometimes works satisfactorily. There are problems, however. Seldom can one man excel in two specialties or find time to do two jobs. Even if an editor is equipped to handle a camera, and tries hard to do so, there is always the risk that his talents are being spread too thinly over too many activities. If so, neither his editing nor his photography will be top flight.

3. The third, and ideal, solution to the problem of obtaining good pictures is to add a competent and experienced photographer to the staff. In most cases, the publication will absorb all the cameraman's time; if it does not, the photographer takes on additional duties ranging from making pictures for technical reports to producing training movies or films for methods engineers. But such activities are only side lines; his first loyalty and primary responsibility is to provide the editor with well executed pictures which state a fact, convey an idea, or register a policy point.

16. Distributing the Publication

1. PROMOTING AN ISSUE

Even though a publication is well conceived and superbly executed, it is a wise practice to draw attention to it by a systematic program of promotion and publicity.

How important this final task is for any periodical is indicated by the newspaper advertisements with which the fantastically successful *Reader's Digest* publicizes articles in a forthcoming issue, and by such phenomena as *Life*'s promoting itself with a large display in *Look*.

Industrial editors can also profitably stimulate reader anticipation of things to come, usually by adopting all or some of the following practices:

1. In each issue of the publication, run a box or article announcing highlights of the next issue. An interesting variant is to run a short quiz asking five or six interesting questions about major subjects to be covered in the next issue.

2. Produce and circulate posters which announce, *"The News—Out Friday."*

3. Develop bulletin-board displays drawing employee attention to special feature articles presented in the forthcoming issue.

4. If the organization has a supervisory newsletter or other written communication with lower echelons of management, insert an item describing the next publication's content. Some managements go one step further and supply supervision with advance copies of issues containing especially important articles. The object in both cases, of course, is to prepare the supervisor either to answer employee questions or to initiate discussion of important stories.

2. DISTRIBUTING THE PUBLICATION

After producing and promoting the employee periodical, one vital, final step remains: to get it into the hands of its readers. There are two principal ways to do this job. One is to distribute the issue on the organization's own premises, either in the employee's work area or at the exit gate. The second way is to mail the publication to employee homes.

Surveys find that advocates of manual pick-up and those of mailing are equally divided.

Managements who distribute the publication on the premises generally do so from motives of economy. Savings in postage per issue may range from one to several hundred dollars. For economy reasons also, managements usually try to avoid distributing an issue of the publication to employees at times when they are actually working; experience shows that large numbers of man-hours are spent in reading on the job if this is done.

Thus, distribution generally takes place "at the gate." Portable display racks, protected against the weather, are moved into position at building or plant exits. Signs announcing the issue are posted over the display, and, as employees pass on their way to the parking lot, they pick up their copies from the stack.

Admittedly, there are loopholes in such a distribution system. The most important matter of all—getting the paper into the employee's hands—is left to chance. And there is a second possible pitfall: even if each employee does pick up his copy, the publishers cannot control the eventual destination of the paper. Management simply does not know whether the employee takes his publication home, or whether he reads it en route and discards it before arrival.

Because these basic matters are left in doubt, many managements conclude that the only sure way to distribute the publication is to mail it. Their point of view was summed up cogently by one manager who said, "It's doubtful economy to spend a $1,000 and then fail, for $75 more, to make sure that the publication gets to the people it's intended to reach."

Certainly when a publication is mailed, there can be no doubt that each employee gets a copy and that the paper enters the home where employee families also have a chance to see it. Reader surveys show that mailed issues may have as many as four or five readers, including the employee, his wife, their children, in-laws, and neighbors.

Ultimately, of course, there is no hard-and-fast rule to cover all cases. If a publication is worth doing, no stone should be left unturned to insure its success. But whether a management hands out its publication or mails it should be determined by its own knowledge of, and experiences with, its employee audience.

3. THE COMMUNITY AUDIENCE

A publication is designed primarily to appeal to employees, but that does not mean that its circulation is restricted to company people. Most organizations, even the smallest, endeavor to get added mileage from the employee periodical by using it as a channel to pipe information and favorable impressions to town and community audiences.

For example, a check of 30 typical publications found that copies mailed to non-company people totaled as much as 15 to 20 per cent of total circulation. One magazine serving an employee group of 90,000 had a total distribution of 150,000 copies.

In making up their community mailing lists, such publications begin by focusing upon all local "opinion leaders," such as teachers, ministers, and civic officials. They also include professional people such as lawyers, doctors, and dentists, and they send copies to any site where townspeople are likely to congregate and read: to libraries, YMCA's, clubs, barber shops, and beauty parlors. In addition, most mailing lists will include such interested community audiences as the company's local suppliers or customers, the Chamber of Commerce, management associations, or other business organizations.

Finally, the town newspapers, radio and TV stations should always receive copies of an employee publication. Often, the press finds it the source of worth-while material about the company and its people, and sometimes the business editor will find the germ of a special feature he may want to expand and develop.

All such extra coverage is valuable and should actively be sought. The price of extra copies is minimal, representing principally the cost of the paper required to print them, plus postage. And the circle of people exposed to the information and ideas which management desires to disseminate is enormously increased.

17. Summary

The multiplication of employee publications is an industrial symptom of a profound sociological change which has taken place in nearly every aspect of our society: the rise of large organizations as the characteristic way by which human needs are served. In the past century, U.S. population has grown more than six times; some 17 states have been added to the Union; and the agrarian economy which prevailed through the first two thirds of the nation's life has been transformed into an urban, industrial society of great productivity and awesome complexity. The artisan's shop and the rural craftsman have been superseded by huge mass production and distribution organizations; teeming universities and consolidated schools; complex scientific teams; enormous church bodies; agricultural and social service groups whose memberships span the continent—these are other signs of our times. On all sides, we pool effort and resources to achieve mammoth feats of production and service.

In industry, as in education, science, or the church, the rise of large organizations has created human problems, the most serious of which is maintaining the identity and recognizing the contribution of the individual in a world which increasingly must turn to the group for progress.

Today, top leadership in a business enterprise is often physically remote from the bulk of its people. The close personal relationships which existed between the owner and employee of an earlier time have largely disappeared. The daily interchange of news, information, and opinion which was once common is now rendered impossible by the mere size of the organization and the number of people it contains. As the distance between the top and bottom of an organization increases, the enterprise easily takes on an abstract and impersonal air, building an employee feeling of personal isolation and diminishing his sense of his individual worth, purpose, and achievement. In such a situation, the possibilities for misunderstandings, frustrations, and animosities become enormous.

Yet nothing is clearer than the fact that no enterprise can be more vigorous, efficient, and productive than the individuals who compose it. If the individual lacks a proper understanding of the organization and the conviction that he has an honorable and respected role within it, the enterprise is in for trouble.

Thus, leadership in every organization must devise substitutes to restore as best it can the employee pride and sense of common purpose that came naturally in a time when "management" and "labor" were persons rather than abstractions. It becomes necessary to institute a program of information which will pursue two over-all goals: (1) help the individual to identify himself with his organization and take pride in its achievements, and (2) enlist the support of members in realizing organization goals.

Basically, such a program will rely upon a well-trained supervisory force. It will also include meetings, bulletin boards, letters, handbooks, motion pictures, and allied channels. And, in recent years, thousands of organizations have adopted the employee publication as a primary medium to inform their people and overcome the communications problems posed by physical scale.

There can be no doubt that a well-planned employee periodical can render great service in providing a direct line from management to every corner of the organization. It enjoys many unique advantages: first, it can provide employees with information on an enormous range of subjects which the supervisor may have neither the time nor the knowledge to cover. Second, the publication can insure that, however large the organization, every individual gets the same facts, the same interpretation, the same discussion of management's point of view on the enterprise's problems and needs. Just as important, the publication goes into the employee's home and the complete and authentic information it provides is thereby made available to the individual's wife who often plays a large role in shaping her husband's outlook and opinions. Finally, and most important, readership surveys in most companies indicate that employees are intensely interested in their publications. Because a periodical deals with "my company," "my plant," "my job," "my friends," "my problems," it gets through. It is read.

Concentration upon the many excellent things an employee publication can do well, however, must be seasoned by the recognition that it cannot do everything. If a management is to avoid disappointment, it must make certain before it launches its periodical that its expectations are realistic.

For example, to perform with maximum effectiveness, a publication must be issued into an organization climate of good faith and mutual confidence. If there is no sem-

blance of trust and respect between management and employees, all communication will be difficult; what the publication says, like information emanating from any other management source, is likely to be distorted or resisted, however compelling and factual the message may be.

By the same token, a publication cannot by itself solve deep-down organization problems of discord and friction. It is only a channel of information, an adjunct of actual physical efforts by leadership to change the conditions which have created hostility. Words cannot heal a breach caused by objective situations.

Likewise, a publication cannot change a man's mind overnight, if only because habit plays so huge a role in human affairs. New ideas are absorbed slowly, and alteration of old ones is achieved only over a long period of time.

A final, important realization is that the impact of an employee publication can never be measured with the slide-rule precision of a production process. When dealing with employee opinions and attitudes, management is entering a highly intangible realm. Instances where it can be said without qualification that "the publication did this" will usually be rare.

Ultimately, therefore, a management can justify a publication only by imagining the consequences if it made no attempts at all to keep employees informed about the organization and its needs. It can speculate about what would happen if it trusted to rumor, the grapevine, the union, the political leader or someone else to interpret management policies and motives. After such reflections, a management can only use its best judgment to say, through the publication, the kind of things which it believes will improve employee relations and advance the welfare of the enterprise.

Once a management has decided to produce a publication, how does it insure that it gets the best return on its money? What procedures does it follow to obtain a publication of unquestioned value to the organization?

The first and most important step is to decide clearly and without equivocation what it wants its publication to do. That is, management must establish concrete publication objectives, preferably in the form of a master plan which will guide the editor at every stage of planning and production. Every article and feature which appears in print will then contribute to achieving a significant publication purpose, and there will be no aimlessness or waste in the periodical's pages.

After having defined objectives, the second step to a valuable publication is to employ vigorous, qualified personnel to perform the editorial function. The importance of this step is easily overlooked and many management periodicals over the past 20 years have been weakened because of a compromise at this point. But time has clearly shown that, in publications as elsewhere, management's most important investment is in people. The employee publication is always a direct reflection of the intelligence, imagination, knowledge, and ability of the man who produces it. The editor is the publication.

When objectives are clearly defined and competent personnel assigned to create the final product, any employee publication is well on its way toward a successful career. To be sure, there are many matters which will still have to be settled: the editor will have to be located so that he has access to information and to top management's point of view; a format must be chosen; a budget established; printers and engravers contracted for; and distribution and mailing methods determined. But all such problems are relatively easy to resolve once the publication's destination is decided and a qualified captain is installed at its helm.

Undoubtedly, organizations in every field will grow larger to meet society's needs in the years to come. In business as elsewhere, organization publications will multiply to help solve the expanding problem of maintaining the individual's identity, pride in, and understanding of, his enterprise. Then as now, however, their usefulness cannot be measured by paper consumed and dollars expended; rather, their value will be determined by the hard thought devoted to their planning, the realism and significance of their content and the professionalism with which they are executed.

Appendix

Appendix

A List of Representative Company Publications

Managements in the process of starting up or revamping a publication are naturally interested in models to follow, and thus rises one of the most common questions in the field: "What are the best publications in the country?"

In the course of writing this book, the author closely examined several thousand employee publications produced by organizations representing nearly every type of industrial, business, and service activity. With perhaps 200 notable exceptions, the publications generally revealed the same deficiency: the absence of clearly defined objectives as represented by concerted, well-planned attempts to interpret their organizations, to discuss company problems candidly and authoritatively, or to provide background upon economic problems which threaten business health.

Whether or not a periodical is distinguished for excellence depends upon its content—upon the quality of its subject matter, and the imagination with which it sets out to attain specific, predetermined management goals. Save for this fundamental principle, there is no absolute yardstick to determine which particular publications are "the best." Individual situations, problems, and needs as well as employee attitudes and general operating climate vary greatly from one firm to another, and this means that each management will have to create a product which is, in some respects, unique. The most practical course, therefore, is to pay particularly close attention to those publications which appear to be striving steadily and successfully toward significant objectives.

To help interested managements begin such a study, there is appended below a sampling of publications well worth inspection and analysis. They are not cited as "the best" nor certainly as the only outstanding efforts in the field. Rather, they are presented as a cross section of good publications which, whatever their formats, exhibit a strong sense of direction and purpose.

Plants or companies whose publication's circulation will be 10,000 or under will profit by a look at such newspapers as the following: *Chase Manhattan News*, Chase National Bank, 57 William Street, New York, New York; *C–I–L Contact*, Canadian Industries Limited, Montreal, Canada; *General Electric News*, General Electric Company, Pittsfield, Massachusetts; *Monongahela News*, Monongahela Power Company, Fairmont, West Virginia; *So Cal Gas News*, Southern California Gas Company, Los Angeles, California; *The Bridge*, General Services Department, E. I. du Pont de Nemours & Company, Inc., Wilmington 98, Delaware.

Representative publications in the magazine format with circulations of 10,000 or under are *195 Magazine*, American Tel & Tel Company, 195 Broadway, New York, New York; *Scope*, Mercy Hospital, Baltimore, Maryland; *Pipeliner*, El Paso Natural Gas

Company, El Paso, Texas; *Tokheim Progress News*, Tokheim Corporation, Fort Wayne, Indiana.

In circulations larger than 10,000, the format of most publications is almost universally "magazine," although there are a number of notable exceptions including General Electric Company weeklies at such plant sites as Erie, Pennsylvania; Lynn, Massachusetts; and Syracuse, New York; and the *Flagship News*, issued by American Airlines, 100 Park Avenue, New York, New York.

There are many excellent magazines whose circulations range from 15,000 up to as high as 100,000. All of the following use the magazine style of text illustrated by pictures and focus on the employee group, although other audiences such as community leaders, stockholders, and customers are frequently included on mailing lists: *Cyanamid Magazine*, American Cyanamid Company, 30 Rockefeller Plaza, New York, New York; *Hercules Mixer*, Hercules Powder Company, Wilmington, Delaware; *IBM Business Machines*, International Business Machines Corporation, 590 Madison Avenue, New York, New York; *Our Sun*, Sun Oil Company, 1608 Walnut Street, Philadelphia, Pennsylvania; *Skyline*, North American Aviation, Inc., International Airport, Los Angeles, California; *Telephone Review*, New York Telephone Company, 140 West Street, New York, New York; *The Ohio Bell*, Ohio Bell Telephone Company, Cleveland, Ohio; *The Torch*, Standard Oil Company (Ind.), 910 South Michigan Avenue, Chicago, Illinois.

"Picture-Story magazines" — publications whose principal emphasis is upon photographs to which text plays a subsidiary role —are comparatively rare. Three examples worth reviewing are: *Better Living*, E. I. du

Pont de Nemours & Company, Inc., Wilmington 98, Delaware; *Today*, International Harvester Company, 180 North Michigan Avenue, Chicago, Illinois; *WE*, Western Electric Company, Inc., 195 Broadway, New York, New York.

In addition to representative employee publications, many companies may also be interested in reviewing typical "externals." In their purest form, these are designed to sell goods, new product uses, or applications and sales ideas to customers, dealers, or similar groups. The polished and professional way in which such magazines approach their task of selling products is eloquent evidence of the way conscious, clearly articulated objectives unify and give impact to a publication. Five examples from the field: *Dow Diamond*, Dow Chemical Company, Midland, Michigan; *Du Pont Magazine*, E. I. du Pont de Nemours & Company, Inc., Wilmington 98, Delaware; *Service*, Cities Service Company, 60 Wall Street, New York, New York; *Shell Progress*, Shell Oil Company, 50 West 50th Street, New York, New York; *Steel Horizons*, Allegheny Ludlum Steel Corporation, Oliver Building, Pittsburgh, Pennsylvania.

In addition to becoming familiar with publications produced by other companies, managements will also want to be acquainted with the field's two major professional organizations, chapters of which are found in nearly every area of the country. These hold annual conferences, conduct seminars, circulate information on new trends or techniques and generally work to stimulate editors and upgrade publication standards. These organizations are: American Association of Industrial Editors, 40 Carter Lane, Elkins Park 17, Penn.; and International Council of Industrial Editors, 9 Overwood Rd., Akron 13.

Glossary

Glossary

Most technical terms or expressions used in industrial journalism are common to all printing and publishing activity, and definitions may be found in any standard work on newspaper production or typography. Those that management people are most likely to encounter, and those used by industrial editors in a special or unique sense, are defined below.

Anticipation. The process of planning and printing publication material which "anticipates" or looks ahead to possible future problems, misunderstandings, or misconceptions; providing employees with a fund of information on any topic which might become a subject of debate or dissension in the future.

Box. A short, three- or four-sentence item, sometimes a bulletin, and often set in bold type, which attracts special reader attention because it is "boxed" by printers' rules.

Caption. By definition, a heading or overline over a picture, but generally used synonymously with "cutline," or the descriptive text which appears under a photograph.

Communications program. A system of activities by which an organization's leadership seeks to keep employees informed on the operations, problems, motives, goals, or needs of the enterprise. Basically, a business organization will depend upon the person-to-person contacts of supervision to keep employees well informed; in addition, a rounded program usually features an employee publication, and also includes bulletins, personal letters, meetings, motion pictures, bulletin boards, or other media.

Company publication. Used in this work synonymously with "employee publication" (see below); can also be a periodical produced for company audiences other than employees, such as customers, stockholders, etc.

Copy. The text of news stories or feature articles to be set in type. Pictures are also referred to as "photocopy."

Cut. An engraving or metal plate by which a photograph is transferred to the printed page.

Cutline. One or more lines of text run under a photograph to describe its contents or enlarge its meaning; generally run in smaller type than other text in the publication.

Dummy. A diagram drawn by the editor to indicate where each block of text, photograph, and headline will appear in the final publication. A dummy is drawn for each page.

Editorial. A journalistic form in which the editor sheds the traditional role of mere reporter and expresses his personal opinions; he recommends, takes a stand for a point of view, or urges readers to adopt a specific course of action.

Editorial advisory committee. A group of ranking management people in a plant or company appointed to keep the publication editor fully informed of problems and needs of the organization and to advise him on publication policy. See Chapter 10.

Employee publication. A periodical, usually in newspaper or magazine format, produced by a company's management for employees. Its prime purposes are to build the individual's pride in, or identification with, his organization and to win his support for company objectives or programs.

Engraving. See **Cut.**

External. A company publication edited and produced for an audience outside the sponsoring organization. Typical examples are sales promotion or advertising publications beamed at customers.

Feature. An extensive story which gives employees background, insight, or a broader picture of a company news event, policy, or problem.

Filler. One or two sentences reporting a significant fact or statistic related to publication objectives; it is used to "fill" an incomplete column, generally in a newspaper.

Format. The form in which a publication is printed; its shape, size, and general physical makeup; i.e., newspaper format, or magazine format.

Gimmick. A novel idea, fresh angle, or unusual device by which to create or begin a publication feature.

Goal. The purpose a publication, story, or feature is designed to achieve.

Grapevine. The word-of-mouth route by which rumors, gossip, speculation, half-truths and, at times, facts, are circulated through an organization.

House organ. Employee publication.

Identification. Used in this book to signify an individual's feeling of pride, both in his organization itself and in the role and function which he performs within it. To build employee identification is a primary goal of publications. See Chapter 3.

Internal. An organization publication circulated to a company's own people, such as a publication for employees, a supervisory newsletter, etc.

Layout. Used synonymously with "make-up"; the design of a publication, or the way in which text, photographs and art are physically displayed upon the page to make content visually interesting and appealing to the reader.

Layout sheets. See **Dummy.**

Lead. Opening sentences or first paragraph of an article. It will usually register, directly or indirectly, the editor's theme; what follows thereafter will be documentation of his point.

Localize. Adding impact and interest to a story by stressing the subject's pertinence or importance to "local" plant or company people.

Manager's column. A personal column bearing the by-line of a plant or company manager in which employees are provided significant information, insight into management's point of view, analysis of plant or company business outlook, etc.

Master plan. An outline or chart constructed to guide an industrial editor's planning. It usually contains a terse statement of publication objectives, together with a list of story-themes which the editor will stress to achieve those objectives. See Chapter 9.

News. An event, announcement or opinion which is interesting and significant to readers, and thereby worthy of coverage in the publication. The industrial editor usually has to create the bulk of his important news. See Chapter 13.

Objective. A purpose or goal which an employee publication sets out to achieve. Clear definition of objectives is the basic step in producing an effective publication.

Picture story. A story composed of a sequence of photographs which tell a story, make a desired point, or register a predetermined impression. Captions, headlines, and text blocks are subsidiary to the pictures themselves.

Q and A. A type of publication feature in which significant information is presented by means of questions and answers, often in the form of an interview with a high-ranking member of management.

Readership survey. A poll to find out how the publication is being received. The object is not to discover what subjects should be discussed (management determines this), but rather to determine whether the periodical's content is being presented interestingly enough to attract and hold readers.

Recognition. Applauding in print an individual's achievements, or describing his skills, know-how, and personal contribution to the enterprise's success.

Repetition. The first rule for registering important information with readers; usually achieved by running a series of articles which make the same point in a different way.

Run. To use or print an article or picture.

Spread. In newspapers, an article which extends across two or more columns; in magazines, a feature which covers facing pages.

Story theme. A basic point or idea which an article is designed to register with the reader.

Tabloid. The newspaper format most commonly adopted by employee publications; usually, it is five columns wide, roughly 18 inches deep, and contains 4 to 16 pages.

Text block. The written matter, usually short, which accompanies or introduces a picture story.

Validation. Proof of an article's point or contention; usually achieved by use of unchallengeable facts or statistics, or by quoting the opinions of authorities or company experts.

Index

Index